Constructions of Women's Age at the Workplace

Frauen, Forschung und Wirtschaft

Herausgegeben von
Regine Bendl, Karin Heitzmann und Angelika Schmidt

im Namen der
AG Frauen in Forschung und Lehre an der Wirtschaftsuniversität Wien

Band 18

PETER LANG
Frankfurt am Main · Berlin · Bern · Bruxelles · New York · Oxford · Wien

Margret Beisheim/Florentine Maier/
Linda Kreil/Bianca Gusenbauer
(eds.)

Constructions of Women's Age at the Workplace

PETER LANG
Internationaler Verlag der Wissenschaften

Bibliographic Information published by the Deutsche Nationalbibliothek
The Deutsche Nationalbibliothek lists this publication in the Deutsche Nationalbibliografie; detailed bibliographic data is available in the internet at <http://www.d-nb.de>.

Printed with financial support of the Federal Ministry of Science and Research in Vienna.

Proofreading and formatting:
Mag. Meta Gartner-Schwarz and Dr. Ulla Ernst

ISSN 1433-4658
ISBN 978-3-631-57836-0

www.peterlang.de

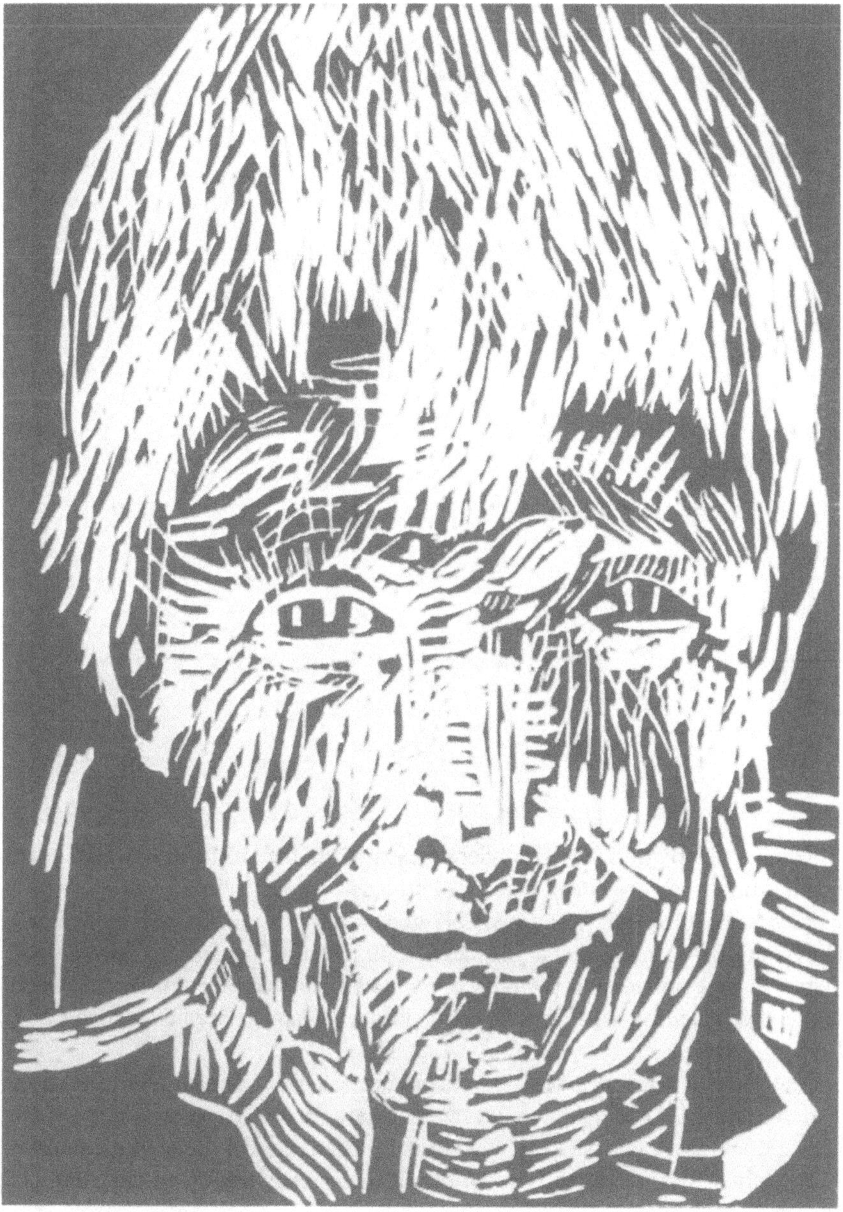

Old Woman (1)
Linoleum Stencil

Old or elderly women are underrepresented in the world of art and in the media. Rarely can one find a portrait of an older woman in an art gallery. Elderly women seem to belong to an invisible generation. The Grand Hall of Vienna's University of Economics and Business Administration houses a gallery proudly displaying the impressive portraits of its past presidents. In the decades since university status has been granted, not a single woman has been appointed to this leading position.

The women's pictures raise questions and ask for a female presence in the portrait gallery. Leadership in western society is still a predominantly male concept, and these portraits can, therefore, be interpreted in socio-political terms. The portraits symbolize the wisdom of old age, archetypical for "The Sage Old Woman".

Greta Znojemsky

Contents

Margret Beisheim

Women's Age as a "Double Jeopardy" – an Introduction

Forever young and carefree while, at the same time, motherly and caring, innocently pretty, sexually alluring, girlish, and wise all at once – women in our society are always constructed with regard to their age. As long as they are attractive and live up to the expectations of the public, as long as they meet social standards (by staying young, being slim and active, etc.), they can play their part in economy. When they get older, however, they drop out of sight and vanish into thin air.

As the title *constructions of women's age at the workplace* indicates, the contributions to this volume can be read with a constructionist framework in mind. Although not all authors take up a constructionist approach, it is what we had in mind when we compiled the volume. There is, of course, no single definition of constructionism that would apply to all the work carried out under this term. Still, if we want to name a key assumption of constructionism, it is that human beings do not perceive the world from an objective point of view, but construct it in co-operation with others as they assign meanings to everything they deal with. We live in a world imbued with meanings that have been transmitted to us by others and that we continue to reproduce – or change.

This also applies to the categories of age and gender. Like any other distinction that human beings make, age and gender are socially constructed, that is to say, they are made salient, and particular meanings are assigned to them through human interactions. Age and gender have no essence of their own; there is no fixed meaning on the basis of biological, historical, religious, economic, or any other reasons. Is strength male and empathy female? Is imaginativeness young and scholarship old? Is one worth more than the other? Our society tends to give particular answers, but these answers can always be questioned.

The contributions to this book are like pieces of a jigsaw puzzle that cover various ways of constructing women's age at the workplace. Together they contribute to a fairly broad picture of how constructions of age and gender work in our society.

The present volume is the result of an international and interdisciplinary conference entitled *fem_research_exchange06* held on October 30th and 31st, 2006 at Vienna University of Economics and Business Administration. The conference stood in a long tradition of feminist research conducted by scholars at our University. It was organized by *Florentine Maier, Linda Kreil, Bianca Gusenbauer,* and *Margret Beisheim* who had formed the *fem_research_exchange_team* and now serve as the editors of this book. The conference was accompanied by an exhibition of artworks with the specific topic "Women and Age" by *Greta Znojemsky*, who has now contributed two pictures reproduced at the beginning and at the end of this book.

If there is one basic assumption that runs like a golden thread through all the contributions to this volume, it is the belief that age is something that matters especially to women. A woman is seldom perceived as "ageless", but is habitually categorized and assessed according to her age. Age-specific expectations exist for her body, her behaviour, and her way of living. In an economic context, these social norms concerning age and ageing have important consequences for women. They affect the way positions (e.g. as employees and consumers), resources (e.g. salaries), and opportunities (e.g. career options) are distributed. What is noticeable, however, is that a woman's age is always held against her: A woman is too young for leadership, too unreliable (in terms of a possible pregnancy) to be promoted, too old to be retained in the company's work force.

Women in our society are often constructed as weak with regard to both their physical as well as their psychological powers. They always look young and friendly and are ever so ready to take over low-paid jobs and unpaid duties. In industries where the majority of employees are female, even the wages of male supervisors are low (cf. Ostroff/Atwater 2003). The very fact that the majority of people working in a certain profession is female (e.g. in child care) drastically reduces employee's chances to receive a better income. This stands in direct contrast to the wages employees earn in technical professions, which still form a male domain.

Women often internalize this kind of discrimination and deliberately withdraw or reduce their claims. Especially for older women in work life, our society has developed stereotypes that work to their detriment: An older female worker is supposed to be frugal and flexible (see Ainsworth 2002, McMullin and Berger 2006). If she complains about being subjected to age or gender discrimination, she risks being labelled as a bitchy old hag. Such stereotypes silence older women and deprive them of their legitimate right to speak. Older women thus become invisible in social life. With this book, we also want to take up the cudgels for bitchy old hags and bring some of the concerns of older – and prospective older – women back into debate. The contributions to this collection aim to shed light on the multiple forms of distinctions – which easily become discriminations – our society creates when roles of women in their different stages of work life are assessed.

For employers and governments, there is a great deal at stake when it comes to the shaping of the working lives of older women. From an economic perspective, the skills and competences of these women will become increasingly important to organisations competing for their labour. Employers need to understand how to create a positive and productive working environment to suit women of different capabilities. Governments need to examine how their policies can enable older women to enjoy their later years. They need to manage two competing objectives: One is to assist women in remaining in the workplace as they age, and the second is to develop financial strategies that enable them to retire when they need to.

Older women – no matter whether they are mothers or not – have often had to take up a disproportionately difficult role in supporting their families and maintaining a work career at the same time. Like others in the community, they deserve the best opportunities to fulfil their personal as well as their career aspirations. There are important questions concerning the next generation of older women that need to be considered now: How long are they to continue to work, or at what age are they to retire? What are their preferred work options as they become older? Which work options will they be able to manage – physically, psychologically, and intellectually? How will their career choices influence their retirement prospects? The situation the next generation will have to face will not be the same as that of the present generation of older women. Their future has not yet been clearly defined. We hope that our investigation of present day perspectives will be of assistance to them in their planning. And, indeed, one of our messages to them is that they need to plan ahead.

The aim of this book is to provide useful information and perspectives to policy-makers who may be able to influence future work, education, and retirement regulations of older women in the workforce; managers, employers, and academics whose attitudes may be crucial in developing new ideas and options for older women at work; and older women themselves and their younger colleagues who may gain new insights from understanding the forces influencing their options and the way in which these can be managed.

In achieving these aims, our first task was to identify some of the theoretical limitations inherent in various concepts of aging and in the manner in which these concepts are interpreted by society. What emerges most clearly is that there is great variability among women and that a woman's date of birth is an unreliable and limiting descriptor of her capabilities and aspirations.

Secondly, we isolated some of the aspirations and experiences of older women in the workforce as well as the factors that influence their work force options. In exploring these issues we did not confine ourselves to the situation in Austria but also included investigations into the issues with which women in Finland and Australia are confronted. What situation do women face in an aging workforce, how much flexibility do they possess, and what issues do they need to deal with?

Our third task was to define the government policies and other contextual factors which can limit or expand the options we take for granted in our home country. As discussed in the chapter by *Helga Eberherr, Roswitha Hofmann,* and *Alexander*

Fleischmann, governments in the EU and elsewhere have – at some stage – begun to take measures that address the specific issues arising from population ageing.

Lastly, we identified some of the developments that may make choices in late work life more interesting and pleasant. We identify ways of how organisations can make work life more acceptable for older women, and offer suggestions as to how women can actively manage their careers with an eye to their future and how the concept of career capital can assist them.

The first chapter in this volume presents different conceptualizations of age and ageing and can also be seen as a framework for the following chapters. *Helga Eberherr, Roswitha Hofmann* and *Alexander Fleischmann* provide insights into the European Union EQUAL project *AGEpowerment* and lay the ground for the discussion on women and age. They do this by showing that age has many different meanings, depending on the given context: We can conceptualize age as a chronological data, as a status quo in a person's life, an ability to work, an indicator for decay and old age, etc. or – in a broader view – as a phenomenon of intersectionality which is linked to gender, ethnicity, and sexual orientation. Ageing in our eyes is not seen as a chronological data but as a process. In the very first chapter, the concept of intersectionality is being discussed. Being female and old at the same time is, after all, a double jeopardy (Onyx 1998).

In the next chapter, *Monika von Bonsdorff, Sirpa Koponen,* and *Iiris Aaltio* raise the question of how older women can be retained at the workplace. She presents a quantitative study on Finnish nurses which shows that retirement plans of older nurses are dependent on the quality of their working conditions.

Irene Kloimüller then examines very similar questions from a practical human resource management perspective. The author presents a framework for active ageing at the workplace from a consultant's perspective. She identifies health promotion, work organization, personnel development, and organizational culture as central criteria that allow active ageing at the workplace and reports the most promising results achieved in a pilot study with nurses in an Austrian hospital based on this approach.

How much are women worth in our society? How are their contributions valued? How come women, when they get older, lose their career aspirations and withdraw from the workplace? The chapter by *Marilyn Clarke, Linley Hartmann,* and *Margaret Patrickson* examines these questions. In particular, they investigate the factors influencing the decisions of older Australian women academics to retire or to stay at the workplace.

Linley Hartmann and *Helene Mayerhofer* discuss older women's career opportunities in the labour markets of Austria and Australia. They look at different forms of career systems, especially at the concepts of the "boundaryless" and "protean career", and demonstrate how women can use concepts taken from contemporary career management to plan ahead and manage their careers.

The contribution by *Linda Kreil* takes up a legal perspective. The author shows that in Austrian labour law, women's age is treated differently from men's age when it comes to dismissals. She shows how age and gender discrimination intersect in Austrian labour law, resulting not in an adding up but in a multiplication of women's discrimination. The author highlights some legal regulations which were once developed to protect women from the strain of the workplace but now assist in discriminating against them.

No matter whether we take an economic, social, or a legal perspective – women are subject to specific role assignments in our society. In the final chapter, *Florentine Maier* undertakes a discourse analysis in a hairdresser's shop, which shows that women have special rules in mind when they obey social constructions of what an older woman should look like in order to be perceived as "decent". She points out alternatives to the dominant discourses of "successful ageing" and "ageing as decay", but also identifies the limitations of the new approach to ageing, which she refers to as "emancipated ageing".

All the contributions to this book in some way aim at de-constructing women's age to uncover women's social circumstances at the workplace – which, after all, can be seen as a mirror of society as a whole.

What *functions* do these constructions of women's age have? Is it only to reduce complexity that we put women into 'boxes' and subject them to stereotypes? Is it the cliché that women have to conform to, the pre-conceived ideas we have in mind when dealing with young and old women? Or is it because women and men alike are afraid of a change of power relations and prefer things to stay the way they are?

Perhaps the demographic changes in the labour market – with a decreasing number of young and a steadily increasing number of older workers as well as a stagnating or diminishing total labour supply – will help to bring about a change in attitudes. Perhaps these economic pressures will be a convincing enough argument that our society cannot afford to fade out a significant part of its members. However, several more years will have to pass until the demographic trend towards an ageing workforce will become fully effective. Moreover, economic and political developments (such as the transferral of jobs to newly industrializing countries and the enlargement of the European Union) may, to some extent, offset the ageing of the labour force. What is more, while the demographic trend points towards a higher labour force participation of (older) women, it says nothing about the quality of this employment, for example with regard to wages, job security, and opportunities for development. We, therefore, cannot sit back and wait for demography to solve all problems for us.

A lot needs to be done to improve older women's roles at the workplace – by employers, political decision-makers, male and female workers of all ages, researchers, teachers, consultants, personnel managers, etc. (Naturally, this enumeration does not imply any order regarding the weight of their responsibility.) With this book we hope to contribute to this momentous task.

Literature

Ainsworth, S. (2002): The 'feminine advantage': A discursive analysis of the invisibility of older women workers. Gender, Work and Organization, 9(5): 579-601.

McMullin, J.A. and Berger, E.D. (2006): Gendered Ageism/Age(ed) Sexism: The Case of Unemployed Older Workers. In: Casalanti, T.M. and Slevin, K.F. (eds.): Age Matters: Re-Aligning Feminist Thinking. New York: Routledge, 201-223.

Onyx, J. (1998): Older women workers: A double jeopardy? In: Patrickson, M. and Hartmann, L. (eds.): Managing an Ageing Workforce, Warriewood, Australia: Woodslane, 88 – 105.

Ostroff, C. and Atwater, L.E. (2003): Does whom you work with matter? Effects of referent group gender and age composition on managers' compensation. Journal of Applied Psychology, 88(4): 725 – 740.

Helga Eberherr, Alexander Fleischmann
and Roswitha Hofmann

Labour Market and Organisational Perspectives on Age(ing) – Bringing Gender, Diversity, and Intersectionality into Focus

1 Introduction

Research on age and ageing in Europe has increased considerably in the last years. Two central concerns of age research are recent demographic developments and scenarios of 'excessive' ageing of the population due to low fertility rates and a steadily increasing life expectancy. On a macro level it is feared that these tendencies will lead to a destabilisation of social security systems. Therefore, on a political level and within the EU administration, much effort has gone into adopting adequate policies in order to deal with these challenges. As part of the Lisbon Strategy specific targets concerning the employment rates of people aged 55 to 64 were set: By 2010, 50% of people aged between 55 and 64 should be active members of the workforce (European Commission 2006). However, statistics (EUROSTAT 2007) for the year 2005 for the European Union (EU 25) clearly show significantly lower employment rates: 33.7% for older women, 51.8% for older men, and 42.5% for the age group as a whole.

Among the EU-25 countries there are substantial differences regarding the labour market participation of older women, which ranges from 12.4% in Malta to 66.7% in Sweden. The goal of increasing labour market participation of older people is a direct response to the predicted ageing of societies. In order to reach this goal, anti-discrimination policies are combined with strategies against social and economic exclusion, which, in turn, will promote Europe's competitiveness and ensure productivity and economic growth.

One measure which forms part of the new employment strategy was the implementation of the EQUAL program as part of the European Social Funds (ESF). The aim of the program was to create within local projects innovative solutions for establishing an integrative labour market. This article reflects the work of the authors in a sub-project of the EQUAL development partnership 'AGEpowerment'[1] implemented at the Academic Unit for Gender and Diversity Management

1 AGEpowerment is an EQUAL development partnership financed by the European Social Fund and the Austrian Federal Ministry of Economics and Labour. The authors of this article

at the Vienna University of Economics and Business Administration. The aim of the sub-project was to provide the development partnership with a knowledge base of scientific findings on age and ageing. In order to do so, the authors had to start with a reflection of structuralist-functional life course models as they are considered to reproduce stereotypical approaches to age and ageing. By looking at the roots of the problem, age-related stereotypes can be identified as a central mode for the persistence of discriminatory processes and structural imbalances on the labour market. The reproduction of stereotypes concerning gender, age, and other dimensions on the macro level of politics, the organizational level, and the individual level had to be analysed. While all these levels were considered, the main emphasis was placed on the organizational level in order to find practicable measures to promote the inclusion and retention of older workers in organizations.

Although discrimination based on age, in some way or the other, concerns all age groups, policies tend to focus either on youth unemployment or on problems related to retirement before the statutory pension age. The fact that there are still gender-specific imbalances on the labour market made it evident that gender had to become a main focus of the project. Women are still subject to age discrimination at an earlier age than men. Therefore, stereotypical dichotomies, like old-young, female-male, etc., had to be questioned. Currently, however, on a political as well as on an organisational level, age – if it is already defined as an issue – is mostly discussed singularly, without contextualizing it with other factors of social division, such as gender, ethnicity, migration, lifestyle, or sexual orientation. This problem has been addressed by adopting social constructivist concepts concerning the relation between gender, age, and other factors of social division in order to allow for intersections between different discriminatory dimensions. As a consequence, the authors' core assumption was that discrimination based on age cannot be eliminated on the different levels unless processes of stereotyping and intersections between different aspects of social divisions (e.g. ethnicity, gender, sexual orientation, class, etc.) have been taken into account.

The following argumentation is largely based on the authors' practical experiences within AGEpowerment and on the theoretical concept that forms the underlying structure of this work. Therefore, the central questions of this article are how to conceptualize age in a non-stereotypical way and how to transform this conceptualization to the organizational level as well as to management practices. As a consequence, the article starts with a discussion of major theoretical approaches to gender and age(ing)[2]. This discussion includes the social constructivist approaches of doing gender, doing ageing, and that of sociological life course

---

participated in the project from July 2005 to December 2006. For more details see www.agepowerment.at.

2 We use the expression "age(ing)" in order to stress the fact that the term "age" does not only refer to a person's chronological age but also to ageing as a process.

perspectives. In order to understand the diversification of life courses in late modern societies and its impact on gender and age(ing) the roles of stereotypes and intersectionality are discussed in section 3. The last section looks at practices which make it possible to transfer the exemplified theoretical framework and our practical experiences onto the organisational level. This suggested management process can be summarized under the expression 'managing ageing'. A summary of our main arguments as well as possible implications of our findings will complete this article.

2 Age(ing) as a Social Process

The construction of age as 'doing age' can be seen in everyday interactions (Laz 1998; Eberherr 2005; see also Coupland, Coupland, Giles et al. 1991) in a similar way as one can observe gender being constructed and maintained, which is described in the well-known concept of 'doing gender' (West and Zimmermann 1987)[3]. Seen from this theoretical perspective, age is constructed with acts of communication, language, symbols, pictures, etc., and it is inscribed in structures and processes. Therefore, age has to be understood as socially constructed within specific contexts. This means that age is connoted differently in different contexts. Conceptualizing age as socially constructed entails that it is always contestable and connected to certain power relations and not a natural or essentialist category. Strongly connected to doing age are processes of stereotyping. Certain assumptions concerning age-groups and classifications formed by a combination of social, cultural, and political influences and beliefs affect the distributions of resources and can lead to discrimination. These processes of construction and their possible contestation happen on the macro, the meso as well as on the micro level.

In the following, major sociological approaches to age and ageing are critically discussed using the aforementioned concept of doing age. Bury (1995) distinguishes between three different approaches. The first one is the structural or political economy approach (e.g. Townsend 1981; Walker 1981; Estes 1986) which focuses on structural imbalances and which Bury criticizes for underestimating older people's agency as well as for disregarding cultural dimensions of ageing. The second one, Laslett's theory of Third Age (Laslett 1989), introduces a division of the human lifespan into four ages, in which the first age is characterized by dependency and education; the second by independence, maturity, and responsibility; the third by personal fulfilment; and, ultimately, the forth age is characterized by final dependency and death. We agree with Bury (1995) in that this approach is highly normative as the Third Age is seen as the one in which activity and fulfilment occurs (something that is impossible for many people in that age

3 West and Zimmermann developed this approach based on works by Garfinkel 1967 and Goffman 1977, 1979.

group, especially for women without a sufficient financial basis) and which stands in contrast to the negative image of the Fourth Age. Indeed, both approaches fail to account for diversity within age groups and neglect the intersection of many axes of social division at any stage in life. The concepts mentioned above are, therefore, not useful for the conceptualization of age in an intersectional frame. Consequently, the authors took the life course perspective (Bury 1995; Featherstone and Hepworth 1989; Kohli 1985; 1986) as one starting point of their project work, since it acknowledges the fact that different biographies are reproduced within structural imbalances as will be explained in the following paragraph.

Classifications based on chronological age (such as 45+ or 50+, etc.) are used in various contexts (e.g. in statistics, to select target groups for employment policies, in advertisements, etc.). In order to modify this theoretical perspective and place it in an intersectional frame, the important question in the light of life course perspectives on age(ing) is whether such classifications actually (re)produce stereotypes. Here it is important to point out that conceptions and meanings of age and ageing are created in a specific historical and social context with the purpose of making biological processes culturally intelligible. According to Saake (1998), this means that we do not age because our bodies or minds want to, but rather because we use the category of age to make changes over time plausible. Our experiences within AGEpowerment showed that, on an individual level, the self-images of people who are addressed by classifications such as the ones mentioned above often do not correspond with images connected to these stereotypes.

From a social constructivist perspective, it is obvious that such classifications are forms or ways of doing ageing. They bear different meanings in different contexts and form the basis of social inclusion as well as exclusion. Tews (1993) has contributed to this discussion with his analysis of "structural changes in ageing". This analysis points to the fact that the increase of life expectancy combined with changes in social arrangements has led to both qualitative and quantitative changes regarding the later years of a person's life. This means that – also due to a prolonged time span in which one is subject to the label 'old' – identity conceptions of 'older people' have multiplied, which calls for greater attention to the new diversity among this so-called 'age group'.

As elaborated above, late modern societies are characterized by a diversification of lifestyles and life courses. The chronologically standardized life course model, defined by sequences and by their corresponding social institutions, dominated modern societies for decades. This model has now been replaced by its de-institutionalisation, as Kohli (1985; 1986) has pointed out, but it still has its relevance as a map of references for individuals to orient and plan their activities. Accordingly, one can identify different 'normalities' for women and men. While 'typical' – and therefore stereotypical – male life courses have traditionally been shaped by paid employment, i.e. a succession of education, paid work, and retirement, female life courses have been far less employment-oriented and have been shaped by the roles of (house)wife and/or mother. This fact still forms the basis of structural disadvantages for women who have reached 'old age', especially since they are confronted with a much higher risk of poverty, as Backes (1993) has demonstrated.

The concept of de-institutionalisation (Kohli 1985) shows that these orientations have lost their importance due to various factors, such as the increase in women's labour market participation and the rise of contingent work (often referred to as 'McJobs') for both women and men, which results in a greater risk of discontinuous (paid) work careers. On the other hand, European social security systems are still based on the ideal of uninterrupted long-term full employment, which is a typical characteristic of male careers. As a consequence, it has become considerably more difficult to re-enter the labour market for those who do not have a seamless succession of full employments, and, in addition, the possibility of establishing a sufficient basis for social security is curbed. This applies to both men and women, although far more women are affected (see e.g. Backes 1993).

Furthermore, women often have relatively low-paid jobs and work in traditionally lower-paid branches of industries. As studies on the distribution of domestic work and caring responsibilities show, women still bear the main burden with regard to these tasks (see e.g. for the U.K. Sullivan 2000). Especially for older women this means an accumulation of social risks as their life courses are often characterized by fragmented work biographies, lower-paid jobs, and a greater emphasis on unpaid work, such as domestic work or caring responsibilities. Similar findings have been reported by Bernard, Itzin, Phillipson et al. (1994), stating that older women's disadvantages in the workplace result from former career breaks (often due to caring responsibilities) and the loss of the "golden decade" in work life (ibid.: 62), which often falls exactly into the time span of their caring responsibilities. On the labour market, being conceived as an older woman constitutes a fatal combination. In addition, parameters, such as ethnicity, sexual orientation, the level of education, etc., can contribute to further discrimination on the labour market. This issue will be addressed and elaborated on in the following chapter.

3 Conceptualizing Age(ing) as an Intersectional Issue

As, for example, Ginn and Arber (1995) argue, the connections between gender and age(ing) need to be made transparent on various levels, thereby allowing for the interweavement of gender and age with other factors of social division, such as ethnicity or class. The present paper shall contribute to this process.

One way of understanding the intersections between age and gender was introduced by the concept of intersectionality, which can be defined as

> ... signifying the complex, irreducible, varied, and variable effects which ensue when multiple axis of differentiation – economic, political, cultural,

> psychic, subjective and experiential – intersect in historically specific contexts. The concept emphasizes that different dimensions of social life cannot be separated out into discrete and pure strands. (Brah and Phoenix 2004: 76)

Knapp (2005a) defines the concept of intersectionality in a similar manner by referring to Weber (2000) claiming that it

> ...stands for an analytical programmatic in policy contexts focusing on multiple discrimination and vulnerabilities, and it stands also for a more general theoretical programmatic by aiming to relate the integrated study of large-scale societal structures of dominance, the historical and contextual systematics of unevenly distributed power, meso-level institutional arrangements and forms of governance, interactions between individuals and groups as well as individual experiences, including the related symbolic processes of representation, legitimating and meaning production. (Knapp 2005a: 255)

As can be seen from these definitions, intersectionality conceptualizes notions of identity and also includes the macro level as well as the meso level. Currently, intersectionality is a widely discussed issue in academic research (e.g. Klinger 2003; McCall 2005; Knapp 2005a; b; Verloo 2006; Yuval-Davis 2006) but this has not led to more complex differentiations on any of these levels. For example, although the EU has, by now, developed a broad range of policies concerned with anti-discrimination and diversity issues (Squires 2005), these policies hardly refer to intersectionality when dealing with multiple inequalities (Verloo 2006: 211).

Verloo identifies three major problems with regard to intersectionality in the EU. First, the current policy needs to be questioned, since it proclaims a similarity between the different axes of discrimination and addresses them with the same measures while, at the same time, differentiating between inequalities by providing different policy attention and different levels of protection. Second, the EU directives are not far reaching enough as they do not work in favour of a "diversity mainstreaming or equality mainstreaming" (Verloo 2006: 215). Third, these policies lead to an "increasing competition between inequalities" and the establishment of various hierarchies among them. Verloo (2006: 222) concludes that

> ... there seems to be a wide range of dimensions that differentiate between unequal social categories. It seems wise to ground policy strategies not only in the similarity, but also in the distinctiveness of inequalities. Moreover, these inequalities are not independent, since there are many historical, political, social and cultural intersections.

As outlined in section 1, the EU identifies various 'target groups', or indeed 'problem groups' on the labour market, also in relation to age and gender. Although this may have sound reasons, from a critical point of view it does in fact reinforce age stereotypes[4]. In the group discussions we conducted in AGEpowerment with women aged 45 to 64, a variety of possible identification categories other than age emerged. Participants reported that they did not identify with 'their' age. This can be seen as a sign of resistance against what Butler calls "the

4 For a similar discussion on the perpetuation of gender roles see Hirschauer 1994, 2001.

temporary totalization performed by identity categories" (Butler 1993: 230), indicating that to describe a person in single terms can never mirror social realities.

The act of grouping individuals by assuming a certain degree of similarity between them is based on stereotypes and, therefore, constructs a misleading homogeneity, which eliminates the perspective of wide-ranging differences between individuals. In our group discussions with women who were identified as the 'target group' (unemployed women aged 45 to 64), the main differences discussed were those based on ethnicity (often referred to as being identified as 'foreign' because of a certain non-native accent) and those resulting from different life courses. Consequently, it is necessary to look at ageing as an intersectional process, at age as a concept which has different meanings in different contexts, and at certain hegemonic conceptions of life courses. One way of counteracting the tendency to reproduce stereotypes by forming seemingly homogenous groups is to raise awareness within work organisations. Regarding the aim of the EQUAL project AGEpowerment this meant that we had to search for management tools which are sensitive towards age(ing) and gender and which, at the same time, can be transferred to other diversity factors. We could thus counteract reproducing stereotypes by forming 'problem groups' within an organisation. Our approach will be presented in the next section.

4 Management Sensitive to Age(ing) and Intersectionality

As outlined above, doing age and the reproduction of age-related stereotypes also take place on the organizational level. Accordingly, this opens the possibility for new management practices to deal with ageing in a constructive and non-discriminatory way. However, the current discussions on ageing as well as its implications have not yet reached the mainstream of small and medium-sized enterprises (SME), as the project work in AGEpowerment has shown. However, as a study by the European Commission (2005) indicates, there seems to be some awareness among larger companies which have already implemented diversity management, as 39.1% of these organisations address the category 'age', which makes it second to the category 'gender' with 42.3%.

Indeed, one can see that not including diversity among age groups is a common weakness of many management books and guidelines dealing with older employees, since this means that they are treated as a monolithic group. Bearing in mind the definition of intersectionality provided above, however, it is obvious that the source of the problems needs to be identified and discussed in order not to work with only the symptoms (discrimination in its different forms). Therefore, we suggest that the focus should lie on intersections "in historically specific contexts" (Brah et al. 2004: 76). For new approaches within organisations this would require to look at specific situations, rather than developing measures with stereotypical images in mind. As a result, we call for approaches that confront this problem by emphasizing the diversity of age(ing) in connection with other dimensions (e.g. ethnicity, disability, sexual orientation, etc.). In an effort to 'mainstream' diversity, our approach tries to focus on introducing non-stereotypical perspectives on diversity in everyday business processes, as will be outlined in the following sections of this article.

4.1 Why Manage Age(ing)?

Literature on age management (at least that by German speaking authors) often starts with defining problems that might emerge when companies do not identify the potentials older employees possess. Very often, the negative scenario described to raise readers' awareness is the prognosis of dramatic changes in the population's age composition over the next years, which, in turn, leads to changes in the composition of the workforce (Fasel and Kailer 2001; Heyer and Henkel 1995; Morschhäuser, Ochs and Huber 2003).

Closely connected to this is the prediction that it will become difficult to recruit (young) skilled personnel. It is usually suggested that the solution to these problems can be found in age management. However, the picture conjured up here is already stereotyped, as certain age groups are rendered as problematic. Heyer and Henkel (1995), for example, observe that associations people have with older employees within organisations are highly subjective and depend on the organizational context. Older age is often placed in a positive context and associated with experience when referring to executives, while the negative image of old age (as being a time of decreasing productivity and innovation) is ascribed to employees on a lower level of the hierarchy.

The fact that age can have such divergent connotations has lead to the dilemma age management currently finds itself in. On the one hand, there is the need for individually differentiated approaches to ageing in companies; on the other hand many companies have to be sensitized to the issue of age and ageing. This issue, however, is often dealt with by focusing on *one* problem group only: that of older employees. From the authors' point of view, in order to consider ageing as a process, the central goal of age management must be to sensitize managers and executives to ageing as a process which affects *all* employees. This is also highlighted by studies which have shown that personnel policies towards older employees often do not depend on older employees' actual performance but rather on the pre-conceived *perception* managers have of their performance (Strotmann, Klee and Rosemann 2004: 41).

A well-established tool to sensitize managers and executives (see for example Blum, Becker and Zimmermann 2006) is the 'age structure analysis', which has to be critically discussed reflecting the above theoretical considerations on stereotypes. An age structure analysis measures the age group composition of an organisation's workforce. To get a clearer picture, detailed analyses of age structures on a departmental level and an additional exploration of further characteristics, such as people's educational backgrounds, etc., are proposed (Blum et al. 2006: 44-45). Age structure analyses often use statistical methods to create future scenarios and anticipate future (quantitative) personnel policies.

If one keeps in mind the above discussion on stereotypes and the diverse aspects of age, age structure analysis is problematic for at least two reasons. First of all, age structure analyses can only anticipate quantitative human resource measures (e.g. recruiting or different forms of staff reduction), while qualitative policies, such as vocational education and training, workplace design, or occupational health initiatives (which are of particular importance when dealing with an ageing workforce), are often not considered. Secondly, there is a great risk that analyses based on chronological age explicitly counteract a differentiated approach, since a mismatch of age groups within an organisation might lead to a problematization of one age group – and not to a differentiated view on employees founded on their actual performances, competences, and potentials.

Explorative interviews that were conducted in AGEpowerment showed that companies, after conducting an age structure analysis, actually refocused their personnel policies on *chronological age*, as they tried to counteract imbalances in their age group composition which they had identified in a merely quantitative age structure analyses.

4.2 'Problematic Age' or 'All Ages'?

As ageing is, by definition, a process that affects all people and, hence, all employees of an organisation – no matter what chronological age they are – each and every organisation is confronted with an 'ageing workforce'. Therefore, we suggest that the focus of attention ought to shift from age management towards *managing ageing*. In this chapter we will outline some steps to be taken on the way to an age(ing) sensitive organisation. Krenn (2001: 44-45) distinguishes between those organisational policies focusing on age and those focusing on ageing. While the former are a reaction to shortcomings of the past that are visible in a deteriorating condition and performance of the workforce, the latter concentrate on establishing a sustainable work environment. Consequently, the focusing on ageing means to develop strategies (for short, mid, and long term perspectives) that try to avoid unsafe, unhealthy, and demotivating work conditions for all employees. The range of approaches reaches from focusing on 'marginal groups', as, for example, on 'young' and 'old' employees only (Schmidt 2004: 29), to implementing policies that integrate all generations in an organisation. The former is highly problematic as it, again, suggests that 'special' groups are the problem, without highlighting ageing as a process that affects all employees. Such a procedure fosters well-known stereotypes. In the following chapter we will sketch some *proactive* and holistic approaches to age(ing) which aim at all generations within an organisation.

4.3 Managing Ageing

This chapter summarizes some of the content of the *Guideline for Small and Medium-sized Enterprises* (Eberherr, Fleischmann and Hofmann 2007) that was published by the authors in the course of the EQUAL project AGEpowerment.

Our starting point for conceptualizing measures for managing ageing is the 'Work Ability House' as described by Ilmarinen and Tempel (2003). By extending their approach, we can sketch the house, as seen in figure 1 below.

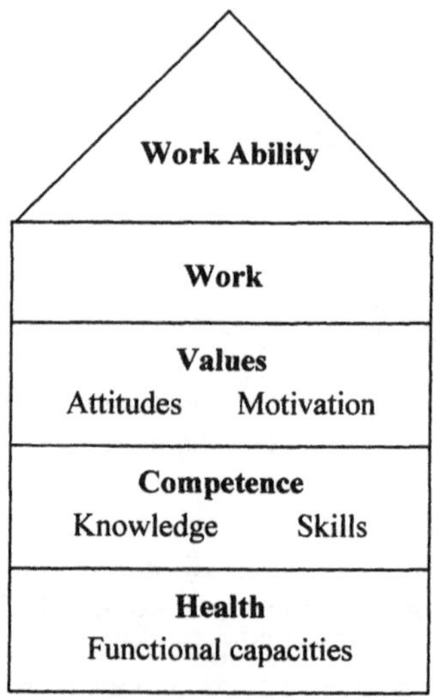

Figure 1: The Work Ability House (an adaptation of Ilmarinen and Tempel 2003: 92)

On the first floor, the term 'health' refers to the employee's physical, psychic, and social health. The first floor can only sustain if competences in the form of knowledge and skills exist on the second floor. On the third floor we find values and attitudes, including those concerning the work as such and the working environment.

We distinguish between four types of measures (following Heyer and Henkel 1995) to create a consistent policy for personnel and organisation development that integrates all employees, no matter what age they are. These four categories are: Organisational Culture, Work Organisation, Occupational Health and Safety, as well as Human Resource Development. As figure 1 demonstrates, all these measures in turn influence to various degrees an employee's health, competences, and values and, as a consequence, help to improve the individual's work ability. Since the above discussion on intersectionality was taken as a framework, the measures described below do not specifically focus on one age group, but rather on establishing an integrative working environment.

Organisational Culture

Central to managing ageing is the establishing of an organisational culture that promotes encouragement, development, learning, and approval. This means to place a strong emphasis on communication and mutual learning in order to eliminate stereotypes and discriminatory conditions. An important starting point is a critical reflection on organisational wording which needs to become sensitive to the intersectionality of age, gender, ethnicity etc. Measures that approach organisational culture include enhancing communication between generations, for example by introducing mentoring programmes, in-house journals, an open-door policy, internal marketing, and opening spaces for communication. The field of organisational culture also includes changes in leadership styles towards more participative forms.

Work Organisation

Part of improving work organisation for both employees and employers are flexible working time schemes. In addition to well-known forms, like part-time or flexitime, long term schemes should also be considered. Such schemes schedule, for example, working time (including sabbaticals) over several years or allow for a yearly renegotiation of working time, holidays (not only the one of the religion which is dominant in a specific organizational context), and salaries. Concerning the organisation of work itself, job rotation, job enlargement, and job enrichment are among the key issues in developing an age and life course sensitive work organisation. Such measures and introducing project-based work in mixed teams (regarding age, gender, ethnicity, sexual orientation, physical abilities etc.) are helpful to promote different perspectives and solutions. This should be conductive to long term motivation and life long learning for all employees.

Occupational Health and Safety

In order to ensure occupational health and safety, it is important to realize that health is not only of significance to the individual employee (her or his personal health condition) but also to the organisation as a whole. Central to the implementation of occupational health and safety are, therefore, *preventive* measures that avoid the deterioration of the employees' health. Indeed, if health is to be understood as comprising physic, psychic, and social components, measures to promote organisational culture, work organisation, and human resource development also have to be taken into consideration as part of an integrative plan for occupational health. A comprehensive health plan should lead to a minimization of work pressure as well as to a decrease in the frequency of employees' medical conditions, which, at the same time, means a reduction of sick leaves, industrial injuries, as well as an increase in productivity for the employer. When it comes to health and safety in the workplace it is important to bear gender-roles in mind. Hegemonic pictures of masculinity often lead to the rejection of health and safety measures by male employees as they might be considered 'unmanly'. For this reason it is often advisable to introduce a health and safety committee that build acceptance and scrutinizes, for example, working processes or even comparatively simple issues like, for instance, the cafeteria menu.

Human Resource Development

The main concern of human resource development lies in vocational education and training, which combines individual education, training plans, and goals with long term career planning – for all employees in all positions. In this context effective tools are appraisal interviews, the introduction of mandatory training times, or the provision of individual training budgets. The training measures themselves do not only include 'classic' training in courses but also the exchange of knowledge between and among younger and older employees. In this case the terms 'young' and 'old' are not understood as referring to a person's chronological age but rather as a reference to the amount of knowledge she or he has accumulated. The transfer of knowledge can be accomplished in combination with the work organisation measures mentioned above, for example through placements, internships, or training on the job. Moreover, recruitment processes have to be reorganized in order to ensure that stereotypes do not govern the recruiting of new employees.

5 Conclusions

As discussed in this article, a diversified life course perspective towards ageing can help to contextualise age(ing) and emphasize heterogeneity and diversity. On a political level this means to seek for policies that bring diversity into the mainstream, a process which Verloo (2006) called "diversity mainstreaming or equality mainstreaming". In order to take this to the organisational level, we have focused on strategies that do not single out certain 'problematic' age groups, but rather work proactively for all age groups by helping employees to maintain the ability to work throughout their whole lives. To summarize, managing age(ing) focuses on establishing a sustainable work environment in the sense of a management framework which is sensitive to age(ing) and intersectionality. Such sensitiveness results in avoiding the reinforcement of stereotypes, which still work as implicit basic assumptions not only on the organizational, but also on the individual and political level. Therefore, we stress the importance of intersectionality of diversity aspects and, thereby, emphasize the heterogeneity within age groups and genders as well as other aspects of social division.

Literature

Backes, G.M. (1993): Frauen zwischen ‚alten' und ‚neuen' Alter(n)srisiken. In: Naegele, G. and Tews, H.P. (eds.): Lebenslagen im Strukturwandel des Alters: alternde Gesellschaft – Folgen für die Politik. Opladen, Westdeutscher Verlag: 170-187.

Bernard, M., Itzin, C., Phillipson, C. and Skucha, J. (1995): Gendered Work Gendered Retirement. In: Arber, S. and Ginn, J. (eds.): Connecting gender & ageing. A sociological approach. Buckingham, Open University Press: 56-68.

Blum, C., Becker, T. and Zimmermann, C. (2006): Altersstrukturanalyse als Instrument zur Personalplanung bei alternder Belegschaft. In: Wächter, H. and Sallet, D. (eds.): Personalpolitik bei alternder Gesellschaft. München und Mering, Rainer Hampp Verlag.

Brah, A. and Phoenix, A. (2004): Ain't I a Woman? Revisiting Intersectionality. Journal of International Women's Studies 5(3): 75-86.

Bury, M. (1995): Ageing, Gender and Sociological Theory. In: Arber, S. and Ginn, J. (eds.): Gender & Ageing. A sociological approach. Buckingham, Open University Press: 15-29.

Butler, J. (1993): Bodies that matter: on the discursive limits of 'sex'. New York, Routledge.

Coupland, J., Coupland, N., Giles, H. and Henwood, K. (1991): Formulating age: Dimensions of age identity in elderly talk. Discourse Processes 14: 87-106.

Eberherr, H. (2005): Was heißt hier alt? Alter(n) im Spannungsfeld Arbeitsmarkt und Lebenswelten. Koryphäe (38): 28-31.

Eberherr, H., Fleischmann, A. and Hofmann, R. (2007): Alter(n)svielfalt im Betrieb. Strategien und Maßnahmen für eine nachhaltige Unternehmenspolitik in kleinen und mittleren Unternehmen. Vienna, Guideline published by the EQUAL project AGEpowerment.

Estes, C. (1986): Politics of ageing in America. Ageing and Society 6(2): 121-134.

European Commission (2005): The Business Case for Diversity – Good Practices in the Workplace Luxembourg, Office for Official Publications of the European Communities.

European Commission (2006): Attract more people into employment and modernise social protection systems. http://ec.europa.eu/growthandjobs/areas/fiche08_en.htm. Visited: 12 Oct 2006.

EUROSTAT (2007): Employment rate of older workers (total, female, male). http://epp.eurostat.ec.europa.eu/pls/portal/url/page/PGP_QUEEN/PGE_QUEEN_TREE?screen=welcomeref&open=/&product=EU_MAIN_TREE&depth=1. Visited: 19 April 2007.

Fasel, G. and Kailer, N. (2001): Ältere Arbeitnehmer/innen – Last oder Chance. Leitfaden zur Entwicklung und Nutzung der Kompetenzen älterer ArbeitnehmerInnen. Wien, WIFI Österreich.

Featherstone, M. and Hepworth, M. (1989): Ageing and old age: Reflections on the postmodern life course. In: Bytheway, B., Keil, T., Allat, P. and Bryman, A. (ed.): Becoming and Being Old: Sociological Approaches to Later Life. London, Sage.

Garfinkel, H. (1967): Studies in ethnomethodology. Englewood Cliffs, NJ, Prentice Hall.

Ginn, J. and Arber, S. (1995): 'Only Connect': Gender Relations and Ageing. In: Arber, S. and Ginn, J. (eds.): Connecting gender and ageing: a sociological approach. Buckingham, Open University Press: 1-14.

Goffman, E. (1977): The Arrangement Between the Sexes. Theory and Society 4: 301-331.

Goffman, E. (1979): Gender advertisements. Cambridge, Mass., Harvard U.P.

Heyer, K. and Henkel, H. (1995): Älter werden im Betrieb. Risiko und Chance. Eschborn, RKW.

Hirschauer, S. (1994): Die Soziale Fortpflanzung der Zweigeschlechtlichkeit. Kölner Zeitschrift für Soziologie und Sozialpsychologie 46(4): 668-692.

Hirschauer, S. (2001): Das Vergessen des Geschlechts. Zur Praxeologie einer Kategorie sozialer Ordnung. Geschlechtersoziologie. Sonderheft der Kölner Zeitschrift für Soziologie und Sozialpsychologie: 208-235.

Ilmarinen, J. and Tempel, J. (2003): Erhaltung, Förderung und Entwicklung von Arbeitsfähigkeit. In: Badura, B., Schnellschmidt, H. and Vetter, C. (eds.):

Fehlzeiten-Report 2002. Demographischer Wandel. Herausforderung für die betriebliche Personal- und Gesundheitspolitik. Berlin, Springer: 85-99.

Klinger, C. (2003): Ungleichheit in den Verhältnissen von Klasse, Rasse und Geschlecht. In: Knapp, G.-A. and Wetterer, A. (eds.): Achsen der Differenz. Gesellschaftstheorie und feministische Kritik II. Münster, Westfälisches Dampfboot: 14-49.

Knapp, G.-A. (2005a): Race, Class, Gender: Reclaiming Baggage in Fast Travelling Theories. European Journal of Women's Studies 12(3): 249-265.

Knapp, G.-A. (2005b): Traveling Theories: Anmerkungen zur neueren Diskussion über "Race, Class and Gender." Fragen an die Geschichtswissenschaften. Österreichische Zeitschrift für Geschichtswissenschaften. 1: 88-111.

Kohli, M. (1985): Die Institutionalisierung des Lebenslaufs. Historische Befunde und theoretische Argumente. Kölner Zeitschrift für Soziologie und Sozialpsychologie 1: 1-29.

Kohli, M. (1986): Gesellschaftszeit und Lebenszeit. Der Lebenslauf im Strukturwandel der Moderne. Soziale Welt, Sonderband 4: 183-208.

Krenn, M. (2001). Erfahrungswissen als Ressource für altersgerechten Personaleinsatz - Neue Wege zu höherer Beschäftigungssicherheit für ältere ArbeitnehmerInnen. FORBA Forschungsbericht 4/2001. Wien, FORBA.

Laslett, P. (1989): A Fresh Map of Life: The Emergence of the Third Age. London, Weidenfeld & Nicolson.

Laz, C. (1998): Act Your Age. Sociological Forum 13(1): 85.

McCall, L. (2005): The Complexity of Intersectionality. Signs. Journal of Women in Culture and Society 30(3): 1771-1780.

Morschhäuser, M., Ochs, P. and Huber, A. (2003): Erfolgreich mit älteren Arbeitnehmern. Strategien und Beispiele für die betriebliche Praxis. Gütersloh, Bertelsmann Stiftung.

Saake, I. (1998): Theorien über das Alter. Perspektiven einer konstruktivistischen Alternsforschung. Münster, Opladen.

Schmidt, V. (2004): Diversity Dimension Alter. Der demographische Wandel als Erfolgsfaktor für das Personalmanagement. Düsseldorf, VDM Verlag.

Squires, J. (2005) Diversity: A Politics of Difference or a Management Strategy? http://www.socsci.auc.dk/forskerskole/pdf-filer/judith%2520squires.pdf. Visited: 13 Sep 2006.

Strotmann, H., Klee, G. and Rosemann, M. (2004). Zur Situation älterer Arbeitnehmerinnen und Arbeitnehmer in Baden-Württemberg – Eine empirische Analyse bestehender Beschäftigungshemmnisse aus Arbeitgeber- und Arbeitnehmersicht, Stuttgart, Wirtschaftsministerium Baden-Württemberg/ IAW.

Sullivan, O. (2000): The Division of Domestic Labour: Twenty Years of Change? Sociology 34(3): 437-456.

Tews, H. P. (1993): Neue und alte Aspekte des Strukturwandels des Alters. In: Naegele, G. and Tews, H.P. (eds.): Lebenslagen im Strukturwandel des Alters. Opladen, Westdeutscher Verlag: 15-42.

Townsend, P. (1981): The Structured Dependency of the Elderly: A Creation of Social Policy in the Twentieth Century. Ageing and Society 1(1): 5-28.

Verloo, M. (2006): Multiple Inequalities, Intersectionality and the European Union. European Journal of Women's Studies 13(3): 211-228.

Walker, A. (1981): Towards a Political Economy of Old Age. Ageing and Society 1(1): 73-94.

Weber, L. (2000): Understanding Race, Class, Gender, and Sexuality: A Conceptual Framework. New York, McGraw-Hill.

West, C. and Zimmerman, D.H. (1987): Doing Gender. Gender & Society 1(2): 125-151.

Yuval-Davis, N. (2006): Intersectionality and Feminist Politics. European Journal of Women's Studies 13(3): 193-209.

Monika E. von Bonsdorff, Sirpa Koponen and Iiris Aaltio

Staying in Working Life? Early Retirement Intentions among Public Sector Nurses

1. Introduction

Health care all over the world, but particularly in Europe, is facing new challenges because of the changing age structure of our societies. The workforce is ageing rapidly due to two fundamental demographic forces: rising longevity and falling birth rates (Patrickson and Hartmann 1995; Ilmarinen 2001; Peterson 2001). As patients age, they require an increasing amount of hospital care. At the same time, there is an increasing shortage of nurses, due to the low number of new nurses entering the workforce, nurses changing to other professions, and nurses retiring early (Minnick 2000; Buchan 2002; Hasselhorn, Tackenberg and Müller 2003; Hasselhorn, Müller and Tackenberg 2005; Simoens, Villeneuve and Hurst 2005). The situation in Finland is especially challenging, since only very few health care professionals come from abroad to work here. Besides, more and more nurses and doctors are leaving Finland after graduating to work, for example, in Sweden, Norway, or England. The reasons for their departure can vary from higher salaries to greater professional autonomy.

All over the world nursing has traditionally been a strongly female-oriented profession. Finland is no exception to this: 90% of Finnish nurses are women. The average age of Finnish nurses is higher than that of nurses in other European countries. A large European study, the Nurses Early Exit Study (NEXT-Study), showed that, compared to other European countries, with 33.1% Finland has the highest proportion of nurses over 50 (Hasselhorn, Müller and Tackenberg 2005). This is not particularly surprising, as the Finnish workforce is generally one of the oldest in Europe. The standard retirement age for nurses in Finland is 63, but it is possible to continue working until the age of 68 (Finnish Centre for Pensions 2007).

The possibility of continuing to work after the official retirement age has put employees' intentions of staying on at work in the centre of early retirement studies (Forma, Tuominen and Väänänen-Tomppo 2006). In this study we focus on nurses' early retirement. We assume that the intention to retire and the intention to continue working stand in contrast to each other. Early retirement has been widely studied and it has been established that both personal factors as well as environmental forces influence an employee's decision to retire (Beehr 1986;

Taylor and Shore 1995; Adams and Beehr 1998). This decision is the outcome of careful consideration and it is preceded by the intention of retiring early.

According to previous studies, pay satisfaction and other organizational factors have an influence on an employee's decision to continue working, rather than retiring early (Cotton and Tuttle 1986; Miceli et al. 1991; Currall et al. 2005). Nevertheless, there are indications that a satisfactory salary might not be the most influential factor in keeping employees at work. Studies have also suggested that making working life more attractive to the ageing workforce might prevent health care employees from retiring early (Minnick 2000; Elovainio et al. 2005; von Bonsdorff, Koponen and Salminen 2006).

The continuous changes in work organization can easily create an imbalance between employees' well-being at work and their feelings of competence. For example, a job characterized by rapid technological changes might lead to an employee's skills becoming obsolete, which in turn might make retirement more attractive (Beehr 1986). A key factor for changes in the work environment is probably leadership behaviour in organizations (Arvonen and Pettersson 2002). Several studies have indicated a connection between leadership behaviour, job satisfaction, and organizational commitment (Lok and Crawford 1999; Pool 1997) as well as the effect of these factors on intentions to leave the profession or to retire early (Grieffeth, Hom and Gaertner 2000; Stordeur et al. 2003).

Nursing, like other health care professions, tends to be both physically and mentally demanding for employees. Especially with regard to older nurses, their workload has to be taken into consideration more carefully (Tuomi et al. 2001; Ilmarinen 2002). Studies have shown that, with both men and women, health-related problems have a significant impact on the decision to retire (Beehr 1986; Taylor and Shore 1995; Adams and Beehr 1998; Shultz, Morton and Weckerle 1998). Gender differences in connection with early retirement have mostly been studied in either all male or all female samples, and the findings of these studies have been inconsistent (Talaga and Beehr 1995; Beehr and Bennet 2007). In order to study gender differences in early retirement, it is necessary to obtain data simultaneously from both male and female employees. In this study, we explore early retirement intentions, while, at the same time, bearing in mind that nursing, as a profession, is female-oriented. The study results will later be evaluated with respect to gender.

The context in which the retirement transition occurs has varied over the years, depending on, for instance, economic changes. These changes have an effect on culturally grounded expectations of the "right" time to retire for each cohort (Moen 1996). Nearly all western countries have to deal with the ageing of their workforce. Retirement legislation in Finland is renewed every five to ten years; the most recent changes were made in January 2005. These most recent changes in the pension scheme were initiated by the realisation that there was insufficient funding for future pensions as well as by the desire to encourage employees to continue working longer. A flexible retirement plan, financial benefits for those who decide to continue working, and improved working conditions were introduced. The new government programme in Finland, which was set up in the spring of 2007, highlights the need to ensure a sufficient number of nursing professionals in the future (www.goverment.fi). This is a clear indication of political awareness of the challenges brought on by global ageing. In the light of these recent changes in retirement legislation and in view of the present interest in developing both rewarding management practices as well as, on a more general level, the overall quality of working life, this study set out to explore how these practises were related to nurses' early retirement intentions. More specifically, we wanted to study

- the various retirement intentions nurses had and
- organizational as well as human resource management factors that were related to these early retirement intentions.

We also believe that by focusing on health care professionals, who are mostly female, we will promote a basic understanding of the gendered nature of this field of work. Questions focusing on late retirement in this particular field might have special implications that have not been taken into account in investigations concerning both men and women. We ask what factors seem to encourage women's later retirement, and what kind of reward system and leadership style are needed among health care professionals if nurses are to be encouraged to remain in the workforce past the official retirement age.

The theoretical and contextual background of the study presented in the next section will be followed by a detailed description of the study and its findings before finally the study results will be evaluated in the light of previous studies.

2. The Background of the Study

2.1 Early Retirement, Employee Health, and Gender

Early retirement is a form of job withdrawal, and it has been defined as leaving a position or career path of longer duration (Hanisch and Hulin 1990, 1991; Feldman 1994). Early retirement concerns ageing employees, and the decision to retire early is preceded by intentions of early retirement (Beehr 1986). Most of the research to date considers early retirement to be a process, which begins with early retirement intentions and ends with adjusting to the new phase in life, brought on by the decision to withdraw permanently from working life. Theories related to adapting to retirement as a life course transition, on the one hand, and to satisfaction with life after retirement, on the other, might offer some background for understanding, predicting, and putting early retirement intentions into a broader perspective. According to Atchley (1989), individuals who preferred to sustain an active level of satisfying social contacts earlier in life, will most likely continue to do so after retirement. The work environment offers a natural way to engage in social interaction with colleagues, supervisors, and clients. For some individuals, the wish to maintain this social network might affect the decision to continue at work instead of retiring early, although social contacts can, of course, also be engaged in outside work. The decision to retire early is not always voluntary: it rather is a matter of choice or chance in the antecedents of retirement (Gould 2006). In this study, retirement is clearly considered a matter of choice, as Finland's public health care system is suffering from a constantly deepening shortage of potential employees.

Physical health and mental well-being are central aspects of an employee's ability to work. Work ability has been conceptually defined as consisting of two parameters: how good the worker is at present and will be in the near future and how capable he or she is of doing his or her job with respect to the demands of the job and his or her physical and mental resources (Ilmarinen, Tuomi and Seitsamo 2005). The promotion of work ability includes taking a worker's health, functional capacity, and competences as well as work demands, the environment, and work organization into consideration (Tuomi et al. 2001). The work ability of ageing employees, especially between the ages of 52 and 58 years, tends to decline dramatically (Ilmarinen and Tuomi 2004). Undoubtedly, this has an effect on early retirement and several studies have shown that health-related problems cause employees to consider early retirement (Beehr 1986; Feldman 1994; Taylor and Shore 1995; Adams and Beehr 1998; Kim and Feldman 1998; Shultz, Morton and Weckerle 1998; Shultz and Wang 2007). One way to address employees' physical and mental capacities with regard to age is to explore how they see themselves in comparison to others in the same age group. This would offer a broader perspective on age, which extends beyond chronological numbers. In their study on successful ageing, Uotinen, Suutama and Ruoppila (2003) found that the perception of personal ageing was related to self-perceived mental and physical well-being.

The role of psychosocial factors at work has become more significant since Karasek (1979) introduced the Job Demand – Control model. Closely related to this concept is the employee's chance to influence his or her immediate work environment. Nevertheless, according to Elovainio et al. (2005), only a few studies so far have concentrated on job control and early retirement. Their study found that both job demand and job control independently predicted early retirement, even when adjusted to age, gender, education, and self-rated health (Elovainio et al. 2005). Another study on Finnish local government workers found that influence at work was one factor that predicted good self-perceived work ability, which in turn predicted early retirement intentions (Tuomi et al. 2001).

Only a few studies have concentrated on gender-related differences in either early retirement intentions or actual retirement decisions (Talaga and Beehr 1995; Moen 1996; Beehr and Bennett 2007). Women in Northern Europe have been active in working life ever since World War II. Since then, it has become necessary to consider possible gender-related differences in the retirement transition. As retirement and pensions are dependent on the length of a person's career, women are easily disadvantaged, as they are seen as children's primary caretakers and, consequently, often have to face sole responsibilities for child-bearing and child-rearing. These responsibilities might result in women entering working life later and having discontinuous work histories. For these reasons, one must consider certain parameters, such as whether they have dependents or what their occupational levels are, as well as their financial and employment status, when investigating employee's retirement decisions (Talaga and Beehr 1995; Beehr and Bennett 2007). According to gender researchers a large section of the public sector is not only dominated by women, it also has a pronounced feminine identity, while the private sector can bee seen as masculine in its identity (Alvesson and Billing 2002). The profitability of the public sector and the social innovations that promote it may be undermined by the comparatively low status associated with it. Changing gender relations means changing the public sector in terms of organizational identity and culture.

2.2 Rewarding and Reward Satisfaction

Rewarding is a central function in human resource management and it typically reflects an organization's culture, its values, and its stage of development. Rewarding should help employees perform their tasks, set their goals, and develop new ways to work (Lahti, Tarumo and Vartiainen 2004, 11). Rewarding is based on an exchange relationship, in which the employee receives different rewards in return for his or her efforts in an organization. These rewards may vary from pay to recognition. From the organizational point of view, rewarding seeks to attract, motivate, and retain employees (Lawler 1990, 36; Armstrong 1999; Gomez-Meija, Balkin and Cardy 2004). Developing a fair rewarding system which is accepted by both employees and management is no easy task.

There are several ways to classify means of rewarding. These means should, ideally, create a motivating and effective total reward system. Financial rewarding includes, besides pay, financial bonuses (e.g. results-based pay), options, stocks, insurance, and retirement benefits (Schuler and Jackson 1996, 417; Armstrong 1999). Non-financial rewards have only come to the attention of managers and organization experts in recent years. There has been a shift towards recognizing the importance of motivating and retaining employees by means other than financial ones (Rynes, Gerhart and Minnette 2004). Non-financial rewards might be meaningful job assignments, job security, praise and recognition, as well as possibilities for personal growth (Schuler and Jackson 1996, 417; Armstrong 1999). Non-financial rewards aim to strengthen employees' commitment to their organization, whereas financial rewards seek to promote high results and productivity (Gomez-Meija, Balkin and Cardy 2004). In health care the supervisor's means to develop financial rewards are limited compared to the multitude of non-financial rewards he or she can employ. Many of the non-financial rewards can be used quite effectively, provided the supervisor acknowledges the importance of such rewards.

Rewarding and employee reward satisfaction are of great interest to the management. Rewarding is one of the biggest expenses in organizations and in knowledge-intensive organizations it is typically the biggest one. The aim of rewarding and of having a reward system is to exert an influence on the employees' motivation, productivity, and commitment to the organization. According to studies, reward satisfaction increases productivity and organizational commitment and leads to a low turnover of employees, whereas reward dissatisfaction is linked to low productivity, job dissatisfaction, tardiness, a high turnover of employees (Miceli and Mulvey 2000; Currall et al. 2005), and sometimes even theft (Greenberg 1990). As we can see, rewarding has a significant effect on an organization's success as well as on the well-being of its employees.

Reward satisfaction, or more commonly, pay satisfaction has been widely studied in recent decades. The best known scale for measuring pay satisfaction is the Pay Satisfaction Questionnaire (PSQ), developed by H.G. Heneman and Schwab (1985). The scale is based on equity theory as well as on the discrepancy model, both of which emphasize pay satisfaction in terms of fairness and an equitable relationship between effort and rewards. PSQ was the first scale to recognize the multidimensional nature of pay satisfaction (Judge 1993). Since 1985 PSQ has been widely used and thoroughly validated (Mulvey, Miceli and Near 1992; Judge 1993; Judge and Welbourne 1994). In recent decades, however, working life has changed and, therefore, it has become important to include a separate measure for pay increase satisfaction in the pay satisfaction scale (R.L. Heneman, Greenberger and Fox 2002). Modified in such a way, it now provides an accurate picture of employee reward satisfaction.

Age has an effect on the employee's reward preferences and reward satisfaction. Prior studies show that preferences shift from pay rises to other benefits and, at the same time, become more diverse as employees age (Doering, Rhodes and Schuster 1983). Although research on reward satisfaction and ageing is scarce, existing studies offer mixed results on whether or not there is a connection between age and reward satisfaction (Doering, Rhodes and Schuster 1983, 135-137). Our recent study focusing on public health care shows that nurses were dissatisfied with their rewards, especially with their pay. Nurses under 35 years of age were more satisfied with trends in their pay than those belonging to older age groups. Nurses over 54 were more satisfied with the consistency of pay determination than younger nurses (von Bonsdorff, Koponen and Salminen 2006).

The Finnish government has reacted to the ageing workforce's intent to retire early by a change in legislation. The 2005 changes in retirement legislation aim to keep ageing employees at work by raising their pensions according to the time they spend working after the official retirement age. Retiring early also has a significant negative impact on the amount of pension that will be received in the years to come. Studies, however, have shown that financial means of rewarding might not be the most effective ones when aiming at keeping employees at work longer (Minnick 2000; Elovainio et al. 2005), although different opinions have been put forward with regard to this matter (Cotton and Tuttle 1986; Miceli et al. 1991; Currall et al. 2005). An adequate salary and financial rewards are still widely seen as effective means to keep employees working. Total rewarding, which takes ageing employees into consideration, is surely an effective means to tackle the forthcoming lack of employees (Van Dalen and Henkens 2002; Hasselhorn, Müller and Tackenberg 2005).

In Finnish public health care rewarding has traditionally been pay-oriented. Tehy, the Union of Health and Social Care Professionals, is the major trade union for trained practitioners of health with over 112 000 registered nurses as members. Tehy has the right to negotiate on behalf of the professional groups it represents (www.tehy.fi/in_english). Hospitals follow the collective labour agreements, which determine wage settlements, maximum working hours, holidays, etc. Public sector pay rises have traditionally been determined by the number of years served in the organization. Usually, ageing employees have been working longer than younger ones and hence are paid substantially higher salaries.

In the autumn of 2004, the way in which salaries of local authority workers were determined changed drastically. Due to these changes employees' salaries now consist of two independent parts: One part is based on the difficulty of the job and the other on personal factors (Commission for Local Authority Employers 2005). The changes regarding the wages of local authority employees, including nurses, are intended to make work more motivating and to permit the effort one puts in one's work to exert an influence on one's salary (Commission for Local Authority Employers 2005). Nurses' wages are largely composed of a basic income (64-81%), which is based on an assessment of the demands of the specific work. The other part is composed of personal factors (8-22%), which comprise work experience, individual competence, and work performance (Statistics Finland 2004; Commission for Local Authority Employers 2005).

2.3 Change-oriented Leadership

In today's world, change is an ordinary, everyday aspect of every organization. Organizations are facing demands for change by the changing environment, by global competition, and by continuously developing technologies. Leadership has been identified as strategically important in a process of change (Kotter 1995).

The tri-dimensional leadership model adds the dimension of change to classic bi-factorial (structure-/task- and relation-/consideration-oriented) models (Ekvall and Arvonen 1991). This change-oriented leadership behaviour dimension depicts a supervisor who creates vision, accepts new ideas, makes quick decisions, and encourages co-operation (Ekvall and Arvonen 1991). In accordance with transformational leadership theories (Bass 1990), change-oriented leadership with its focus on continuous development is based on visionary leadership (Ekvall and Arvonen 1991). Change-oriented leadership shows some striking similarities with Bass's definition of transformative leadership style in terms of "intellectual stimulation" (Arvonen and Pettersson 2002).

It has been alleged that transformational leadership, i.e. enhanced leadership performance, increases, for example, employees' trust as well as their confidence (Bass 1990), satisfaction, and organizational commitment (Bass 1990; Podsakoff, Mackenzie and Bommer 1996). Without transformational leaders, sustainable healthcare reform is not possible (Block and Manning 2007). Other studies, however, have presented findings which strongly contradict such predictions of the effects of transformational leadership. For example, Arvonen (1995) has reported a positive correlation between change-oriented leadership and mental fatigue. Podsakoff, Mackenzie and Bommer (1996) have identified a positive relationship between intellectual stimulation and role conflict.

3. Method

3.1 Sample, Setting and Procedures

Data for this study were collected in a Finnish University hospital. The study population consisted of full and part-time, permanently and temporarily employed, registered nurses, including mental and practical nurses (N = 937). This specific hospital provides special health care for the over 860 000 people living in the health authority district. Questionnaires addressed to these nurses were sent out in December 2006 and January 2007. The nurses participating in the study worked in the surgical or psychiatric wards. Nurses holding a managerial position were excluded from the study.

The response rate of the study was 54.4% (n = 510). The study design allowed the researchers to analyze the demographic data (age, gender, form of employment, and current ward) of the non-respondents. No statistically significant differences were detected between respondents and non-respondents in terms of demographic data, which meant that no systematic bias occurred among the nurses participating in the study. All statistical analysis was carried out with SPSS (14.0).

The majority of the respondents were female (82.9%). The mean age was 41.5 (s.d. 9.7) years, and ages ranged from 21 to 62. Respondents were grouped into four age groups based on previous studies, which focused on age-related changes in employees' physical capacities (National Programme on Ageing Workers 2001; Ilmarinen 2002) and on the average retirement age of Finnish nurses. The age groups were: under 35-year-olds (n = 146), 35 to 44-year-olds (n = 153), 45 to 54-year-olds (n = 155), and those aged 55 and older (n = 56). Nurses were asked to report the number of children they had and the variable was classified as follows: nurses with no children (28.5%) and those who have children (71.5%). Some three-quarters of the respondents (n = 384) were permanently employed, whereas 120 nurses were temporarily employed. The majority of the nurses worked in shifts (73.8%), which is typical of the nursing profession. The length of time the nurses had spent working in the nursing profession (work experience) was controlled for. The nurses had an average of 14.4 years of work experience in the nursing profession, and it was significantly correlated with nurses' age (r = 0.769, p = 0.01). Work experience was divided into four categories according to quartiles (0-4 years, 5-10 years, 11-18 years, and 19-36 years of work experience).

Nurses working in surgical wards (71.2%) and those in psychiatric wards (28.8%) were somewhat unequally represented in this study. Respondents' educational background was classified according to two groups: (1) College level registered nurse education (9.5%) and (2) Bachelor's degree in nursing (90.5%). Income levels were obtained by asking the respondents about their gross monthly income, which was a little over 2140 € on average. Salaries were divided into four categories (under 2000, 2001-2200, 2201-2300, and 2301 and more).

3.2 Measures

The variables used in this study were selected on the basis of previous studies that have shown connections between early retirement intentions and age, gender, self-perceived health, and job control (Beehr 1986; Talaga and Beehr 1995; Taylor and Shore 1995; Adams and Beehr 1998; Shultz, Morton and Weckerle 1998; Elovainio et al. 2005; Shultz and Wang 2007). A limited number of studies have focused on early retirement and organizational factors, such as the rewarding of employees and different leadership styles. Nevertheless, these studies have indicated that such factors might indeed have an influence on retirement intentions (Beehr 1986; Van Dalen and Henkens 2002; Hasselhorn, Müller and Tackenberg 2005).

Self-perceived physical age was measured on the basis of a single question, in which participants were asked if they felt themselves to be physically younger, the same age, or older than other people of their age (Uotinen, Suutama and Ruoppila 2003). Self-perceived health was measured with the help of questions taken from the Work Ability Index, WAI (Tuomi et al. 1998). This index has been thoroughly validated and it has been widely used to measure employees' self-reported health. In this study, three items were used that concerned employees' physical and mental health capacities in relation to their current work and their capacity to continue working in the same profession for a further period of two years. Nurses' opportunities for job control was measured by using an eight item scale, partly based on Karasek's Job Demand – Control model (Lehto 1996). The nurses were asked about their opportunities to determine their working methods, work pace, working hours, etc. The number of respondents, means, standard deviations, and Cronbach alphas are presented in Table 1.

Variables	*n*	*Mean*	*sd.*	*Cronbach alphas*	
Self-perceived physical age	507	1.72	0.58	-	(Scale 1-3)
Self-perceived health	501	4.19	0.76	0.824	(Scale 1-5)
Job control	494	2.18	0.56	0.825	(Scale 1-4)
Reward satisfaction	495	2.27	0.68	0.780	(Scale 1-5)
Change-oriented leadership	494	4.18	1.13	0.964	(Scale 1-6)

Table 1: Number of respondents, means, standard deviations, and Cronbach alphas for variables included in the logistic regression analysis

Reward satisfaction was measured according to a seventeen item scale based on the Pay Satisfaction Questionnaire created by H. G. Heneman and Schwab (1985) and further developed by R. L. Heneman, Greenberger and Fox (2002). For this study the scale was modified to consist of four different elements: pay satisfaction, pay rises, pay administration and structure, as well as non-financial rewards. Likert-type questions were used, such as: "How satisfied are you with your net salary, the way your salary is developing, your pay rises, your chances of influencing pay rises, the recognition you receive from your supervisor, and the consistency in which wages are determined in your organization?" A sum variable was formed, first for each of the four elements concerning reward satisfaction, and then for overall reward satisfaction.

Subordinates' evaluation of the behaviour associated with change-oriented leadership was measured with a Farax questionnaire from the CPE Leadership Model designed by Ekvall and Arvonen (1991). The questionnaire comprises three scales: production, employees, and change-oriented leadership. The change-oriented leadership scale contains four subscales. A leader who displays this leadership style is a promoter of change and growth, has a creative attitude, is a risk taker, and has visionary qualities. Examples of items from each scale in the above mentioned order are: "initiates new projects"; "encourages thinking along new lines"; "makes quick decisions when necessary"; and "gives thought to and makes plans for the future". Items were rated on a Likert scale from 1 to 6.

Early retirement intentions were measured with the help of two separate questions. The first one was health-related, while the second one reflected a relatively unspecific intent to retire as soon as possible (Table 2).

Items	*Yes*	*Maybe/ Missing*	*No*	*Total n*
Do you feel that your health will allow you to work until the age of 63?	141 (51.8%)	(238)	131 (48.2%)	510
I will retire as soon as possible	243 (61.2%)	(113)	154 (38.8%)	510

Table 2: Measures, means, and standard deviations for early retirement intentions

Only respondents stating a clear intention to either continue at work or to retire early were included in this study, even if this meant losing a significant number of respondents. We were interested in nurses who had a strong opinion on the subject, as they can then serve as better proxies for people facing early retirement. Both of the variables were dichotomized for the logistic regression analysis. There was a statistically significant difference between the respondents to the two early retirement questions, which indicated that we were dealing with two separate groups of retirees ($\chi^2 = 18.33$, df = 1, $p<.001$).

4. Results

Two sets of logistic regression models on the relationship between nurses' early retirement intentions, reward satisfaction, and change-oriented leadership are presented as a result of this study. Nurses' self-perceived health was entered in both of the original regressions, but then excluded from the second regression. This was done in order to get a better idea of the role that other factors besides self-perceived health played in the models, as self-perceived health significantly increased the odds of early retirement intentions.

The outcome factor, early retirement intentions, was health-related in the first model, whereas the second one shows relatively unspecified early retirement intentions. In both of the models demographic measures (age, gender, number of children, and shift work), self-perceived physical age in relation to others in the same age group, job control, reward satisfaction, and change-oriented leadership were included. Results clearly showed that nurses' health-related as well as their unspecific early retirement intentions were both differently related to the factors mentioned above. In the following both logistic regression models are described in detail (see Table 3 and Table 4).

	Model 1 including all variables		Model 2 excluding self-perceived health	
Indicator	Odds ratio	95% CI	Odds ratio	95% CI
Age	n.s.		1.58	1.14-2.18
Gender (Categorical)	2.83	1.08-1.31	5.07	2.10-12.24
Number of children (Categorical)	3.50	0.67-0.12	2.45	0.81-0.21
Shift work	5.26	0.48-0.08	5.71	0.38-0.08
Relative physical heath	3.58	1.76-7.27	4.80	8.59-2.68
Self-perceived health	10.10	0.20-0.05	-	
Job control	n.s.		2.05	0.88-0.27
Reward satisfaction	1.88	0.93-0.30	2.45	0.67-0.25

Table 3: Two models on health-related early retirement intentions
(Note: At entry, n = 252, CI = Confidence Interval)

	Model 1 including all variables		Model 2 excluding self-perceived health	
Indicator	Odds ratio	95% CI	Odds ratio	95% CI
Age	1.38	1.06-1.79	1.56	1.22-1.99
Gender (Categorical)	n.s.		n.s.	
Number of children (Categorical)	2.66	1.54-4.60	2.63	1.53-4.51
Shift work	n.s.		n.s.	
Self-perceived health	1.58	0.89-0.45	-	
Job control	1.71	0.89-0.39	1.81	0.83-0.37
Change-oriented leadership	1.32	1.07-1.63	1.28	1.04-1.57

Table 4: Two models on unspecific early retirement intentions
(Note: At entry, n = 371, CI = Confidence Interval)

Health-related Early Retirement Intentions

The outcome factor in the first model was dichotomized into two categories according to whether or not nurses had health-related early retirement intentions.

A significant number of respondents stated that their health would not allow them to continue working until the age of 63 (n = 131). Respondents who were uncertain about whether they wanted to retire or not (n = 238) were excluded from the study. Previous studies offered us guidance in constructing the logistic regression models (Beehr 1986; Talaga and Beehr 1995; Taylor and Shore 1995; Adams and Beehr 1998).

Several demographic variables were included in the model. The final model only contains statistically significant variables. We excluded non-significant variables, such as form of employment, marital status, work experience, professional education, number of dependents in the household, and pay level. In the first phase, in addition to demographic variables, we added self-perceived health, self-perceived physical age in relation to others in the same age group, job control, and reward satisfaction variables to the logistic regression analysis (see Table 3).

Several variables clearly increased the risk of health-related early retirement intentions among nurses. The predictive power of the variables is indicated in terms of multivariate odds ratios and 95% confidence intervals. Age turned out to be statistically non-significant in terms of increasing the odds of early retirement intentions, whereas gender proved to be significant. Some 207 out of the 252 nurses were female, which left us with only 45 men in the model. Compared to men, women were nearly three times as likely to have early retirement intentions. The number of children was also connected to early retirement intentions, which indicated that having children increased the odds of early retirement intentions (OR = 3.50, CI = 0.67-0.12). Nurses working in shifts were more than five times more likely to have early retirement intentions than daytime workers.

Self-perceived physical age in relation to others in the same age group and poor self-perceived health both proved to be related to early retirement intentions. Perceiving oneself to be physically the same age as others or older than them increased the odds of early retirement (OR = 3.58, CI = 1.76-7.27). As far as self-perceived health was concerned, moving one category further towards perceiving one's health to be poor increased the likelihood of early retirement intentions more than tenfold. Reward satisfaction, or rather dissatisfaction, on a scale from one to five had a similar effect (OR = 1.88, CI = 0.93-0.30). In logistic regression analysis, no actual percentage of the variance a model accounts for is reported, although some approximation measures are widely used. In this model R-squared estimates were 0.62 (Nagelkerke $R^2 = 0.624$).

Next, a similar model to the previous one, which, however, excluded self-perceived health, was formed (see Table 3). Results showed that health had a significant impact on retirement: It caused all other variables in the model, except having children, to become more significant. In terms of age this meant that moving from a younger age group to an older one increased the chances of early retirement intentions by one and a half. Low job control was also found to increase the odds of having early retirement intentions (OR = 2.05, CI = 0.88-0.27). Excluding self-perceived health appeared to enhance the significance of reward dissatisfaction with regard to early retirement intentions.

Unspecific Early Retirement Intentions

Like in the previous model, the outcome factor in the second model was dichotomized into two categories according to whether or not nurses wanted to retire as soon as possible. More than sixty per cent of the nurses (n = 243) stated that they wanted to retire as soon as possible. As with the previous model, nurses who were uncertain about whether they wanted to retire or not (n = 113) were not included. After excluding several non-significant demographic variables (e.g. marital status, education, work experience, number of dependents, and pay) we included age, gender, and the number of children. In addition to these demographic variables, we added self-perceived health, job control, and change-oriented leadership in the logistic regression analysis (see Table 4).

Several variables, although different from the first model, predicted the nurses' intention to retire as soon as possible. Gender turned out to be statistically non-significant in terms of predicting nurses' early retirement intentions, whereas moving from a younger age group to an older one increased the odds of early retirement (OR = 1.38, CI = 1.06-1.79). The number of children was related to nurses' early retirement intentions in so far as having no children increased the odds of early retirement (OR = 2.66, CI = 1.54-4.60). The lower the job control, the more likely it was for nurses to have early retirement intentions (OR = 1.71, CI = 0.89-0.39). Self-perceived health also played a role in this model, even if the odds ratio for poor health was not as high as in the first model (OR = 1.58, CI = 0.89-0.45). The more change-oriented leadership the nurses recognized, the higher the odds were for early retirement (OR = 1.32, CI = 1.07-1.63). In this model, the Nagelkerke R-squared estimate was somewhat low at 0.14,

As with the previous model, self-perceived health was excluded from the logistic regression. Results showed that health had an impact on retirement intentions, albeit not an as significant one as in the previous model. This is understandable, since early retirement intentions in the first model were specifically health-related. Excluding self-perceived health enhanced the significance of most of the factors that were previously found to be related to unspecific early retirement intentions, except for change-oriented leadership, the significance of which decreased. All in all, the R-squared estimates remained rather low in this model.

5. Conclusions and Further Implications

The results of this study show that as many as half of the nurses had either health-related or less specific early retirement intentions. The results suggest that reward satisfaction and change-oriented leadership, along with other health- and work-related factors, were linked to these early retirement intentions. Establishing two separate forms of early retirement intentions as well as the factors contributing to these intentions, provides valuable new information on how to keep ageing employees working longer. More so than other European countries, Finland has recognized the approaching shortages in the workforce and, therefore, strongly encourages employees to work at least until their official retirement age (Ilmarinen 2001; Forma, Tuominen and Väänänen-Tomppo 2006). Current research on early retirement intentions and early retirement decisions has focused on self-perceived health, stress, pay level, and several other work-related factors (Adams and Beehr 1998; Kim and Feldman 1998; Shultz, Morton and Weckerle 1998; Elovainio et al. 2005; Forma, Tuominen and Väänänen-Tomppo 2006; Gould 2006).

According to this study, poor self-perceived health was the most significant factor in increasing nurses' health-related early retirement intentions, and it was also statistically significant in increasing less specific retirement intentions. Several prior studies have found that health has a significant impact on employees' intentions to continue at work as well as on the decision to retire either early or as soon as they reach retirement age (Beehr 1986; Feldman 1994; Taylor and Shore 1995; Adams and Beehr 1998; Kim and Feldman 1998; Shultz, Morton and Weckerle 1998; Shultz and Wang 2007). Due to the fact that health proved such an important factor in determining retirement intentions, we decided to perform two separate logistic regressions on both health-related as well as on unspecific retirement intentions.

The factor of self-perceived health proved to be more closely connected to nurses' early retirement intentions than age. Higher age does not automatically mean that he or she wants to retire, but poor health forces nurses to consider early retirement. Somewhat similar results have been reported by, for instance, Forma, Tuominen and Tomppo-Väänänen (2006) and Gould (2006). Another indicator of the significance of health was the fact that both perceived physical age in relation to others in the same age group and shift work increased the odds of early retirement in both of the models on health-related early retirement intentions.

Gender played a role in nurses' health-related early retirement intentions, in a way that women were far more likely to express the wish to retire. The 45 male nurses in this study were nearly three times more likely to stay on at work than their female colleagues (see. e.g. Gould 2006). The number of children was also linked to early retirement intentions, indicating that having children increased the odds of early retirement intentions in both health-related models. Nurses having no children, on the other hand, were more than two and a half times more likely to have early retirement intentions in both of the models on unspecific retirement intentions. These findings can be interpreted as showing that nurses with health-related problems, who, at the same time, care for children and perhaps grandchildren, were more interested in retiring than nurses with no children. Those caring for children are still, and always have been, predominantly female (Talaga and Beehr 1995). Interpreting the relationship between less specific early retirement intentions and having children proved rather complicated. The fact that nurses who had no children still wanted to retire early might indicate that they were socially active outside the workplace and wanted to pursue other than work-related goals in life (Atchley 1989).

Human resource management practices, such as reward satisfaction, have a significant impact on the success of an organization as well as on the well-being of its employees (Greenberg 1990; Miceli and Mulvey 2000; Currall et al. 2005). Nevertheless, they have never been at the centre of previous early retirement research. Early retirement decisions are influenced by many job-related factors, such as attainment of occupational goals (Beehr 1986; Adams and Beehr 1998). Reward satisfaction, in a broader sense, is a central job-related factor.

The reward satisfaction scale in this study consisted of items other than mere satisfaction with the participants' current pay level (Heneman and Schwab 1985; Heneman, Greenberger and Fox 2002). We found that nurses were relatively dissatisfied with their rewards (mean = 2.27, sd. = 0.68), especially with their pay and pay rises. Furthermore, reward dissatisfaction increased the likelihood of early retirement intentions. In this study it was the only factor related to human resource management practices to have an influence on health-related early retirement intentions. Previous research has shown that elements, such as how pay rises are determined, recognition, opportunities for personal growth, etc., are significant in keeping employees working longer (see Minnick 2000; Van Dalen and Henkens 2002; Elovainio et al. 2005; Hasselhorn et al. 2005). In our recent study on public hospital nurses we found that, along with reward satisfaction, a decrease in work strain, high job control, and work satisfaction reduced early retirement intentions (von Bonsdorff, Koponen and Salminen 2006).

Excluding self-perceived health from the original model enhanced the influence reward dissatisfaction had on early retirement. Excluding self-perceived health from the second model on unspecific retirement intentions did not have a similar effect on the other variables of model, including that of change-oriented leadership. This was no surprise, as the effect self-perceived health had in this model was not very strong to begin with, compared to the first model. The effect of reward satisfaction was statistically non-significant in the second model on unspecific early retirement intentions. The same holds true for change-oriented leadership in the model on health-related retirement intentions.

The nurses recognized a significant degree of change-oriented leadership in their supervisors (mean = 4.18, sd. 1.13). The challenges health care is facing seem to have an effect on supervisors' leadership behaviour. As the workforce ages, change-orientation is not only needed to tackle future problems, but also to solve every-day and routine ones. The more change-oriented leadership the nurses recognized, the higher the odds were for early retirement. This might be a sign of emotional exhaustion and an inability or unwillingness to face the continual changes in the organization.

Research on human resource management and leadership are essential, as both represent skills that organizations and managers can develop and modify in order to keep their ageing employees at work. One possible solution to the current problems in health care could be to develop and implement total reward practices which take age into consideration. Rewarding is closely intertwined with other HRM practices, which should also be developed. Simply paying more money to nurses might not be the solution, as consensus is yet to be reached on the effect financial incentives have on employees' intentions of continuing to work (Van Dalen and Henkens 2002; Hasselhorn et al. 2005).

Our study has yielded the following results:

- Two different kinds of early retirement intentions, health-related and unspecific ones could be identified among nurses.
- Poor self-perceived health, shift work, having children versus having no children, higher perceived physical age in relation to others in the same age group, being a female, and reward dissatisfaction made it more likely for nurses to have health-related early retirement intentions.
- Excluding self-perceived health increased the impact of nearly all other factors in the model.
- Having no children, low job control, poor self-perceived health, higher age, and recognizing more change-oriented leadership in the organization made it more likely for nurses to have unspecific early retirement intentions.
- Excluding self-perceived health from the second model on unspecific early retirement intentions had a moderate impact on all other variables.

Ultimately, the various limitations of this study need to be addressed. First, as the data were reported by respondents, some self-reported bias might have influenced the results. The data used in this study was collected at one particular time in one particular hospital, which makes it difficult to generalize the findings. Obtaining longitudinal data would make it possible to exclude period and cohort effects, which might have had an effect on the results of the present study.

Several implications for future studies have already been identified while presenting this study. As mentioned above, longitudinal data would make it possible to address more complex issues regarding nurses' early retirement intention. Obtaining register-based data on nurses' actual retirement would enable more specific regression analysis of the reasons behind a retirement decision. Further research should also focus on those employees who are undecided as to whether they want to retire early or continue to work. In an attempt to ensure an adequate number of qualified health care employees, this group might be the one to focus on in the future.

Acknowledgements

This study has been supported by the Central Finland Regional Fund of the Finnish Cultural Foundation and by the Finnish Pension Alliance TELA. We are grateful to Raija Gould for her valuable comments on this article.

Literature

Adams, G.A. and Beehr, T.A. (1998): Turnover and Retirement: A comparison of their similarities and differences. Personnel Psychology 51(3), 643-665.

Alvesson, M. Billing and Y. D. (2002): Beyond Body-counting. A discussion of the social construction of gender at work. In: Aaltio, I and Mills, A. (eds.) Gender, Identity and the Culture in Organizations. London: Routledge, 72-91.

Armstrong, M. (1999): Employee Reward. 2nd ed. London: IPD House.

Arvonen, J. (1995): Leadership Behaviour and Coworker Health. A study in process industry. Reports from the Department of Psychology, Stockholm University, no. 801.

Arvonen, J. and Pettersson, P. (2002): Leadership Behaviours as Predictors of Cost and Change Effectiveness. Scandinavian Journal of Management 18(1), 101-112.

Atchley, R.C. (1989): Continuity Theory of Normal Ageing. The Gerontologist 29(2), 183-190.

Bass, B.M. (1990): From Transactional to Transformational Leadership: Learning to Share the Vision. Organizational Dynamics 18(3), 19-31.

Beehr, T.A. (1986): The Process of Retirement: A Review and Recommendations for Future Investigation. Personnel Psychology 39(1), 31-55.

Beehr, T.A and Bennett, M. (2007): Examining Retirement from a Multi-level Perspective. In K.S. Shultz and G.A. Adams (eds.), Ageing and Work in the 21st Century. Mahwah, NJ: Lawrence Erlbaum Associates, Inc., 303-319.

Block, L.A. and Manning, L.J. (2007): A Systematic Approach to Developing Frontline Leaders in Healthcare. Leadership in Health Services 20(2), 85-96.

von Bonsdorff, M., Koponen, S. and Salminen, H. (2006):. Sairaanhoitajat ikääntyvässä työyhteisössä – Koetut johtamiskäytännöt Kuopion yliopistollisessa sairaalassa. Nurses in ageing work communities – Human resource management experienced by nurses in Kuopio University hospital. University of Jyväskylä: Working paper 311/2006.

Buchan, J. (2002): Global Nursing Shortages. British Medical Journal 324(7340), 751-752.

Commission for Local Authority Employers. 2005. http://www.kuntatyonantajat.-fi/modules/. 2007.

Cotton, J.L. and Tuttle, J.M. (1986): Employee Turnover: A Meta-analysis and Review with Implications for Research. Academy of Management Journal 11(1), 55-70.

Currall, S.C, Towler, A.J, Judge, T.A. and Kohn, L. (2005): Pay Satisfaction and Organizational Outcomes. Personnel Psychology 58(3), 613-640.

Doering, M., Rhodes, S. and Schuster, M. (1983): The Ageing Worker. Research and Recommendations. Beverly Hills: Sage Publications.

Ekvall, G. and Arvonen, J. (1991): Change-centred Leadership: An Extension of the 2dimensional Model. Scandinavian Journal of Management 7(1), 17-26.

Elovainio, M., Forma, P., Kivimäki, M., Sinervo, T., Sutinen, R. and Laine, M. (2005): Job demands and Job Control as Correlates of Early Retirement Thoughts in Finnish Social and Health Care Employees. Work and Stress 19(1), 84-92.

Feldman, D.C. (1994): The Decision to Retire Early: A Review and Conceptualization. Academy of Management Review 19(2), 285-311.

Finnish Centre for Pensions. http://www.etk.fi/page.asp?Section=12175. 2007.

Finnish Government. The Government Programme. http://www.valtioneuvosto.-fi/hallitus/hallitusohjelma/en.jsp. 2007.

Forma, P., Tuominen, E. and Väänänen-Tomppo, I. (2006): Finnish Pension Reform and Intentions of Older Workers to Continue at Work. Helsinki: Finnish Centre for Pensions Working Papers 2006: 2.

Gould, R. (2006): Choice or Chance - Late Retirement in Finland. Social Policy and Society 5(4), 519-531.

Greenberg, J. (1990): Employee Theft as a Reaction to Underpayment Inequity: The Hidden Cost of Pay Cuts. Journal of Applied Psychology 75(5), 561-568.

Gomez-Mejia, L.R., Balkin, D.B. and Cardy, R.L. (2004): Managing Human Resources. 4th ed. New Jersey: Prentice Hall.

Griffeth, R.W., Hom, P.W. and Gaertner, S. (2000): A Meta-Analysis of Antecedents and Correlates of Employee Turnover: Update, Moderator Tests, and Research Implications for the Next Millennium. Journal of Management 26(3), 463-488.

Hanisch, K.A. and Hulin, C.L. (1990): Job Attitudes and Organizational Withdrawal: An Examination of Retirement and Other Withdrawal Behaviors. Journal of Vocational Behavior 37(1), 60-78.

Hanisch, K.A. and Hulin, C.L. (1991): General Attitudes and Organizational Withdrawal: An Evaluation of a Causal Model. Journal of Vocational Behavior 39(1), 110-128.

Hasselhorn, H.M., Müller, B.H. and Tackenberg, P. NEXT Scientific Report July 2005, www.next-study.net. 2007.

Hasselhorn, H.M., Tackenberg, P. and Müller, B.H. (eds.; 2003): Working Conditions and Intent to Leave the Profession among Nursing Staff in Europe. SATLTSA, Stockholm, Report no 7: 2003.

Heneman, H.G. and Schwab, D.P. (1985): Pay Satisfaction: Its Multidimensional Nature and Measurement. International Journal of Psychology 20(2), 129-141.

Heneman, R.L., Greenberg, D.B. and Fox, J.A. (2002): Pay Increase Satisfaction: A Reconceptualization of Pay Raise Satisfaction Based on Changes in Work and Pay Practices. Human Resource Management Review 12(1), 63-74.

Ilmarinen, J. (2001): Aging Workers. Occupational and Environmental Medicine 58(8), 546-552.

Ilmarinen, J. (2002): Physical Requirements Associated with the Work of Ageing Workers in the European Union. Experimental Aging Research 28(1), 7-23.

Ilmarinen, J. and Tuomi, K. (2004): Past, Present and Future of Work Ability. People and Work Research Reports 65, pp. 1-25. Helsinki: Finnish Institute of Occupational Health.

Ilmarinen, J., Tuomi, K. and Seitsamo, J. (2005): New Dimensions of Work Ability. In: Costa, G., Goedhard, W.J.A. and Ilmarinen, J. (eds.): Assessment and Promotion of Work Ability, Health and Well-being of Ageing Workers. Elsevier International Congress Series No 1280, 3-8.

Judge, T.A. (1993): Validity of the Dimensions of the Pay Satisfaction Questionnaire: Evidence of Differential Prediction. Personnel Psychology 46(2), 331-355.

Judge, T.A. and Welbourne, T.M. (1994): A Confirmatory Investigation of the Pay Satisfaction Questionnaire. Journal of Applied Psychology 79(3), 461-466.

Karasek, R.A. (1979): Job Demand, Job Decision Latitude, and Mental Strain: Implications for Job Redesign. Administrative Science Quarterly 24 (2), 285-308.

Kim, S. and Feldman, D.C. (1998): Healthy, Wealthy, or Wise: Predicting Actual Acceptances of Early Retirement Incentives at three Points in Time. Personnel Psychology 51(3), 623-642.

Kotter, J.P. (1995): Leading Change: Why Transformation Efforts Fail. Harvard Business Review 73(2), 59-67.

Lahti, C. Tarumo, S. and Vartiainen, M. (2004): Palkkausjärjestelmien kehittäminen Developing Reward Systems. Helsinki: Edita.

Lawler, E.E. III. (1990): Strategic Pay. Aligning Organizational Strategies and Pay Systems. San Fransisco: Jossey-Bass Inc.

Lehto, A-M. (1996): Työolot tutkimuskohteena. Työolotutkimuksen sisällöllistä ja menetelmällistä arviointia yhteiskuntatieteellisestä ja naistutkimuksen näkökulmasta. Working conditions as a target of research. The evaluation of content and method in the study on the working conditions from standpoint of social and feministic research. Helsinki: Statistics Finland.

Lok, P. and Crawford, J. (1999): The Relationship between Commitment and Organizational Culture, Subculture, Leadership Style and Job Satisfaction in Organizational Change and Development. Leadership and Organization Development Journal 20(7), 365-373.

Miceli, M.P., Jung, I., Near, J.P. and Greenberg, D.B. (1991): Predictors and Outcomes of Reactions to Pay-for-performance Plans. Journal of Applied Psychology 76(4), 508-521.

Miceli, M.P. and Mulvey, M.P. (2000): Consequences of Satisfaction with Pay Systems: Two Field Studies. Industrial Relations 39(1), 62-86.

Minnick, A.F. (2000): Retirement, the Nursing Workforce, and the Year 2005. Nursing Outlook 48(5), 211-217.

Moen, P. (1996): A Life Course Perspective on Retirement, Gender and Wellbeing. Journal of Occupational Psychology 1(2), 131-144.

Mulvey, P.W. Miceli, M.P. and Near, J.P. (1992): The Pay Satisfaction Questionnaire: A Confirmatory Factor Analysis. The Journal of Social Psychology 132(1), 139-141.

National Programme on Ageing Workers. 2001. http://pre20031103.stm.fi/english/current/ageprog/index.htm. 2007.

Patrickson, M. and Hartmann, L. (1995): Australia's Ageing Population: Implications for Human Resource Management. International Journal of Manpower 16(5/6), 34-46.

Peterson, P.G. (2001): The Shape of Things to Come: Global Aging in the Twenty-first Century. Journal of International Affairs 56(1), 189-210.

Podsakoff, P.M., MacKenzie, S.B. and Bommer, W.H. (1996): Transformational Leader Behaviors and Substitutes for Leadership as Determinants of Employee Satisfaction, Commitment, Trust, and Organizational Citizenship Behaviors. Journal of Management 22(2), 259-298.

Pool, S.W. (1997): The Relationship of Job Satisfaction with Substitutes of Leadership, Leadership Behavior, and Work Motivation. The Journal of Psychology 131(3), 271-283.

Rynes, S.L., Gerhart, B. and Minnette, K.A. (2004): The Importance of Pay in Employee Motivation: Discrepancies between what People Say and what they Do. Human Resource Management 43(4), 381-394.

Schuler, R.S. and Jackson, S.E. (1996): Human Resource Management: Positioning for the 21st Century. 6th ed. New York: West Publishing Company.

Shultz, K.S., Morton K.R. and Weckerle, J.R. (1998): The Influence of Push and Pull Factors of Voluntary and Involuntary Early Retirees' Retirement Decision and Adjustment. Journal of Vocational Behavior 53(1), 45-57.

Shultz, K.S. and Wang, M. (2007): The Influence of Specific Physical Health Conditions on Retirement Decisions. International Journal of Ageing and Human Development 65(2), 149-161.

Simoens S., Villeneuve, M. and Hurst, J. (2005): Tackling nurse shortages in OECD countries. OECD Health working papers no. 19, DELSA/ELSA/-HEA.

Statistics Finland. 2004. http://www.stat.fi/. 2007.

Stordeur, S., D'hoore, W., van der Heijden, B., Dibisceglie, M., Laine, M., van der Schoot, E. and the NEXT-Study Group (2003): Leadership, Job Satisfaction and Nurses' Commitment. In: Hasselhorn, H.M., Tackenberg, P. and Müller, B.H. (eds.): Working Conditions and Intent to Leave the Profession among Nursing Staff in Europe. SATLTSA, Stockholm, Report no. 7: 2003.

Talaga, J.A. and Beehr T.A. (1995): Are there Gender Differences in Predicting Retirement Decisions? Journal of Applied Psychology 80(1), 16-28.

Taylor, M.A. and Shore, L.M. (1995): Predictors of Planned Retirement Age: An Application of Beehr's Model. Psychology and Ageing 10(1), 76-83.

Tehy. www.tehy.fi/in_english. 2007.

Tuomi, K., Ilmarinen, J., Jahkola, A., Katajarinne, L. and Tulkki, A. (1998): Work Ability Index, Occupational Health Care no. 19, 2nd revised ed. Finnish Institute of Occupational Health.

Tuomi, K., Huuhtanen, P., Nykyri, E. and Ilmarinen, J. (2001): Promotion of Work Ability, the Quality of Work and Retirement. Occupational Medicine 51(5), 318-324.

Uotinen, V., Suutama, T. and Ruoppila, I. (2003): Age Identification in the Framework of Successful Ageing. A Study of Older Finnish People. The International Journal of Ageing and Human Development 56(3), 173-195.

Van Dalen, H.P., Henkens, K. (2002): Early-retirement Reform: Can it and Will it Work? Ageing and Society 22(2), 209-231.

Irene Kloimüller

Ageing at Work from a Woman's Perspective

1. Introduction

Generally speaking, ageing in working life is a wide-ranging and complex subject. Ageing as seen from a woman's perspective adds an additional dimension to this topic. The issue of ageing at work includes two different aspects: the aspect of ageing as a continuous process during working life and that of old or aged employees and workers at work. In this article I will take both aspects into account with particular emphasis on aged women at work. I will also describe successful measures that can be taken to promote active ageing in women. Subsequently, I will supplement these measures with my own model of practice called "Masterly Nursing".

What people consider old, or what is actually meant by the term "ageing", is not generally agreed on, and there is no specific age at which someone is commonly considered an older worker. Some organisations and several studies focus on people older than 55 (e.g. Respect for the Ageing, FIOH, or the U.S. Department of Labor, Women's Bureau) while other studies concentrate on those over 45 years of age (e.g. TEP_Equal Elderly – Erfahrung hat Zukunft). For this article I will build on the definition introduced by Naegele (1992) who distinguishes as follows:

- Workers or employees of 40 years and above are described as aged when working conditions are hard and physical demands high, that is, for instance, in industries like the steel, metal, and construction industries.
- Workers/employees of 45 years and above are called aged due to their decreasing chances of getting new employment on the labour market or of pursuing their vertical careers in companies. A lot of programmes set up by employment services are targeted at the age group of over 45-year-olds.
- Workers/employees of 50 years and above are called aged, if they consider retiring from work or refuse to obtain further education.

It depends on organisational culture and attitudes whether employees/workers are considered old. Of course, it also depends on the prevailing definition of age on the labour market and in work science whether someone is regarded an old employee/worker or not.

When discussing the rather specific concerns of ageing at work, one has to bear in mind, however, that in western societies ageing members of the workforce are by no means a minority: Recent demographic developments in Europe have shown that the population is ageing and the proportion of younger people is shrinking. And what is more, this trend is expected to continue (see for example ILO 2005 and Europäische Kommission 2007: 62ff.) well into the 21st century.

In Austria 1.5 million women are over 50 years of age; this is a fifth of the Austrian population (Bundesministerium für soziale Sicherheit und Generationen 2002). When addressing the topic of older women at work, we need to consider in which sectors these women work. The Austrian labour market is characterised by a strong division between typical male jobs and sectors in which a female workforce predominates. Female-dominated sectors are (Statistik Austria 2007, figures refer to the 2001 census):

- the health and social system (73% of all employees are women);
- the educational system (69% of all employees are women);
- the retail industry (68% of all employees are women);
- the hotel and hospitality sector (59% of all employees are women); and
- other service industries (78% of all employees are women).

In Austria some projects focusing on older women at work (aiming, for instance, to maintain their work ability and other faculties) have recently been initiated. Most of these can be found in the health sector (like the "Masterly Nursing" project), but, in general, there are not many such initiatives. The majority of studies, projects, or programmes deal with unemployed older women (from the Austrian Labour Market Service, one Focus of the Project TEP_Equal Elderly 2005-2007).

2. Productive or Unproductive Ageing at Work

The old-age threshold for women at work lies at around 40 to 45 years. Research and experience, however, have shown that a person's biological age only plays a minor role in determining whether he or she can be considered old or not. Individual differences and, above all, working conditions are much more relevant in relation to ageing at work. Most importantly, however, age does not seem a suitable criterion to judge a person's abilities and competences (Eberherr, Fleischmann and Hoffmann 2006: 6). Unfavourable working conditions that do not consider age differences accelerate the process of ageing. Such unfavourable working conditions comprise (Ilmarinen 1995: 28f.):

- discriminating attitudes of superiors and colleagues towards older employees (older female employees or workers have to cope with discriminating attitudes more frequently than their male colleagues; in the eyes of male superiors men mature and gain experience, whereas women become old and less attractive[1]);

- the restriction of human resources development, learning, job rotation, etc., to certain age groups;
- monotonous and/or intellectually undemanding work;
- and poor organisation of work.

Factors that contribute to an inadequate organisation of the work environment include role conflicts, the lack of control on the part of employees, the lack of recognition and esteem (it has often been observed that women suffer from such discriminating treatment more frequently than men[2]), shift work with night shifts, a poor ergonomic design of the workplace, a dangerous or physically stressful work environment (due to a high risk of accidents, changes in temperature, to name but a few factors), as well as excessive physical work demands (above all static or highly strenuous physical work, lifting and carrying, repetitive movements, bent and awkward work postures, and peak work loads).

To recapitulate, one can say that a woman over 50 years of age, who, for instance, works as a professional cleaner or domestic servant, is likely to age considerably faster than one would expect. These jobs are known for their poor ergonomic working conditions, their high physical work loads, the shift work they involve, the few opportunities to learn or get promoted that are offered, and, of course, the low recognition of this type of work in the eyes of the public.

From the point of view of occupational medicine, ageing does not at all mean a lower work performance, it means having other abilities, experience, and a different kind of work performance. The physical performance sinks (more or less slowly, depending on work demands, individual fitness, and health), psychological (emotional) strengths stay relatively unchanged, whereas, interestingly, socio-mental abilities increase. This concept of changing abilities is called the concept of the heterochronic biosocial dynamic of aging (Rimser 2006: 98).

Older employees have a high level of knowledge, professional as well as personal experience, and foresight provided they find the right working conditions. In other words, in order to develop their socio-mental abilities, older employees have to find suitable working conditions. In politics, science and research, for example, older people – including older women – enjoy high esteem. Nobody would think that older politicians or scientists are less competent than their younger colleagues or that their performance is inferior. Quite to the contrary, what is expected from them is a high level of professional experience and competence.

1 This observation is based on interviews carried out by the author of this article with 20 male employees and 7 female employees of the paper and chemical industries in the year 2005.

2 See above.

Ageing throughout working life is a process of change and development, some to the better, some to the worse. By providing age-conform working conditions and individual training, negative impacts can be reduced significantly and positive factors promoted. This means that there can never be just one concept of an ideal working environment, but working conditions have to vary; they need to be flexible and age-conform, i.e. tailored to meet the varying needs of different age groups.

3. Concepts of Promoting Active Ageing in Women

Most models of age management, personnel development, and health promotion that are applied in practice and aim to promote active ageing have a very similar approach to ageing (Buck and Dworschak 2003). The key issues are always work ability, work interest, and competence. These are essential factors when aiming to retain women in the work process until their regular retirement age and to maintain women's employability. Comprehensive programmes address all or most of these factors. In this chapter I will outline the most important measures such programmes take to promote active ageing in women. I will then add some measures I use in my own counselling activity.

As shown in Figure 1, I distinguish between four organisational levels aiming to promote active ageing.

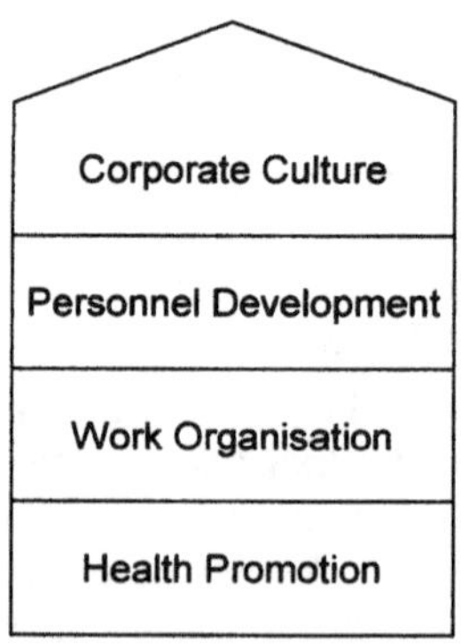

Figure 1: The „Promoting Active Ageing" house

The first level of promoting active ageing involves corporate culture, norms, and attitudes. The aim is to develop positive attitudes towards ageing women, especially among employers and superiors, and raise employee's awareness of the issue. Measures on this level are, for example, positive discrimination programs for women, awarding older women for their experience, the promotion of positive older role models in the company, age-management training for leaders, an active recruitment policy of older women, self-assisting support groups to increase self-esteem of older employees, inter-generational dialogue, dialogue between management and older female employees, and many more.

Level two of promoting active ageing involves personnel development and lifelong learning. On level two the aim is to promote interest in work, competence, and flexibility. Maintaining or increasing qualifications is a very important means of meeting future personnel needs; lifelong learning is an essential prerequisite for achieving a longer working life (Weiler 2005). Apart from learning and competence development, it is also crucial to encourage knowledge sharing and other aspects of personnel and personal promotion. Activities on this level include specialized training at the workplace (such as special training programmes that allow older women to keep up with new technologies), training to improve and adapt existing skills, work-ability training, vocational counselling, etc. The key to success with regard to training and further education is age-adjusted instruction. Age-adjusted training denotes more than simply qualified training. A major concern is that coaches should have positive attitudes towards older trainees. They should be aware of what it means for older employees to learn at their advanced age as well as of the social concepts of learning (older employees, for instance, often have an inaccurate idea of what learning means dating back from their own school days). In other words, older women need to be addressed and motivated differently in order to make them participate in a training programme. They have to understand the purpose as well as the importance of the specific training. Training contents and methods need to be practicable and adapted to their needs. The training should be based upon already existing knowledge and experience. Mentoring or tandem systems by women for women help to promote women. They allow a smooth transfer of cultural and professional knowledge and skills from experienced to inexperienced women. Management by objectives including qualitative objectives (like social goals) help older women to achieve aims and to be appreciated by their fellow employees.

Level three of promoting active ageing focuses on work organisation and on the work environment: On this level the aim is to adjust the work organisation, the work environment, and the ergonomic design of the workplace to the needs of ageing and older employees. There is a wide range of measures that can be taken at organisational level: from competence models, job rotation, and redeployment to the ergonomic design of workplaces. Horizontal career models (also referred to as lateral or competence career models) are often considered part of personnel development. Nonetheless, it seems much more appropriate to place them in the context of work organisation, because they focus on job enrichment and job enlargement resulting from increasing experience and competence.

In the next chapter I will describe such a career model for women (referred to as Masterly Nursing). It was developed for and together with nursing experts of the Wiener Krankenanstaltenverbund (Vienna Hospital Association).

Other models in the area of personnel development focus on job rotation concepts, especially designed for women, or the redeployment of older female employees within a company. Flexible working hours or ergonomic work postures tailored to the needs of older women with health problems are other central issues to promote workability.

On level four, health promotion and individual promotion stand at the centre of active ageing. The aim is to promote work ability, skills, interest in work, health, and well-being on an individual level. Activities range from work-ability training, health promotion programmes tailored to meet the needs of women in general as well as those of certain age groups in particular, and physical fitness programmes to individual counselling.

4. Creating a Career Model Based on Active Ageing: Masterly Nursing, a Perspective for Ageing Nurses

The model which will be described in the following is a good example of measures that can be taken on levels two and three. It organises work, competence development, and learning in such a way that employees/workers of all age groups can achieve mastership. Experienced nurses support younger and inexperienced nurses in their development. The model was presented and published in a report for the Wiener Krankenanstaltenverbund (Vienna Hospital Association) and the Fonds Gesundes Österreich (Fund for a Healthy Austria) by Danzinger and Kloimüller (2001 and 2003).

From 2001 to 2003, based on research on the development of nursing competence, an interdisciplinary team of nurses, psychologists, and personnel experts developed a horizontal or lateral career model called "Masterly Nursing" and tested it in three different hospital wards (a neonatology, a surgery, and a geriatric ward) of the Vienna Hospital Association. 96% of the participants were female nurses, all master nurses were women.

The main aim of the project was to establish a career model on the basis of competence levels. The model should allow nursing staff to develop themselves, their work ability, and their interest in work directly on the job (i.e. when working with patients or clients rather than by switching to teaching or management tasks) and thus to stay longer in their job. Additional or secondary aims were to document the profound knowledge of ageing nurses and their style of working, which is based on and reflects a high level of experience; to develop methods of assessing this knowledge and experience; and to show how much these experienced nurses were appreciated because they stayed in their jobs despite the lack of vertical career prospects.

The project consisted of three phases. Phase 1 involved preparatory research, in order to define competence and experience and to describe how these qualifications change over the years. Ultimately, competence was defined as the ability to perform nursing tasks at different levels and the ability to use knowledge, understanding, as well as practical and social skills to perform efficiently. It consists of individual competence (capability) and core competence. In addition, the development of competence was described in a competence matrix. Interviews with over one hundred experienced female and male nurses and with focus groups comprising about one hundred male and female nurses were conducted to analyse the levels of experience, competence, knowledge, and intuition nurses have.

In phase two the focus lay on developing a career model based on competence levels. This meant that we needed to identify and define:

- the various stages of competence in a nurse's life,
- work contents that are characteristic of these stages,
- the nurse's position and standing within the organisation,
- and his or her coaching and training.

The career model itself was based on the following five competence levels or competence stages:

- beginner,
- advanced nurse,
- competent nurse,
- experienced nurse,
- and expert or master nurse.

Promotion from one to the next competence level takes place by learning from experience, from masterly or master nurses, and by attending external training programmes and formal schooling. Master nurses play a key role in the competence development of the entire team. They develop the practical vocational training for their team based on the team's and on the individual's competence levels. Thus, we are dealing with both learning on the job as well as learning from the job. Ultimately, such a dual system can be seen as an ideal way to promote lifelong learning. Master nurses are experts – with a highly specialised knowledge of nursing, with profound experience, and with a high degree of ethical competence. Professional training is done by the best professionals (i.e. the master nurses) on the job; it, therefore, covers all aspects of competence, and goes beyond mere technical skills.

In phase three first implementation and pilot studies took place in three hospital wards (in the neonatology department with 38 nurses, in the surgery ward with 10 nurses, and in the geriatric ward with 28 nurses) of the Vienna Hospital Association. The practicability of the theoretical model was tested and information was collected on how to implement it on a larger scale. Results of this evaluation showed that age and experience alone do not create masterly knowledge, but that active reflection upon one's strengths and support, for example, by master coaches are of equal importance. They also showed that the model allows promoting competence according to the needs of the target group and, therefore, makes learning relatively easy. As part of the project methods of assessing knowledge and experience on individual as well as on group level, such as a matrix with indicators for social competence, ethical competence, and so on, were developed.

Finally, the pilot study showed that, by implementing this model, nurses, above all nurses in the middle of their professional careers, will continue to work in their jobs and will think less frequently of retiring early. In 46 semi-structured interviews focusing on workability and work interest, which were carried out with nurses of the three wards two years after the first intervention, only 14 people did not think that the project has helped and helps to promote their wish to remain in the same job. Personally, I believe that this model is very attractive, especially to highly qualified nurses who want to continue working with patients. It offers long-term perspectives for the nursing staff based on learning on and from the job and is a good model of lifelong learning.

5. Conclusion

Since recent demographic changes have resulted in a growing proportion of older and a shrinking proportion of younger employees and workers, concepts of promoting the ageing workforce should be brought to the attention of organisations, and respective measures need to be implemented on a large scale in companies. So far, such measures have not taken on a sufficiently large scale and many companies seem to be oblivious to the specific needs of our continuously ageing workforce (see also the article by Eberherr, Fleischmann, and Hofmann in this volume).

Only a few Austrian enterprises run programmes to maintain their workers' work ability and interest in work and, interestingly, the majority of these projects and programmes are not gender-specific. These programmes either focus on gender or on various age groups, but never on both. This is rather surprising, because older or ageing women have very specific demands and need work organisation and a work environment adjusted to their needs.

In order to create a better understanding of ageing women at work and to develop more specific measures to support them, it is necessary to collect more gender-specific data as well as data on specific groups of women, like older migrant workers. Projects should consider the needs of older female employees and workers with regard to work ability, lifelong learning, interest in work, health, and well-being – these being the central pillars of active ageing. It is necessary to identify, present, and promote models of good practice for women on company level. These will help to develop future age-management strategies tailor-made for women and encourage companies to adopt such strategies.

Literature

Buck, H. and Dworschak, B. (eds., 2003): Ageing and Work in Europe, Strategies at Company Level and Public Politics in Selected European Countries, Demography and Employment. Fraunhofer IRB Verlag. Stuttgart. http://-publica.fraunhofer.de/eprints/N-17445.pdf. Visited: Nov. 22, 2007.

Bundesministerium für soziale Sicherheit und Generationen (2002): Chancengleichheit für ältere Frauen. Dokumentation der Tagung vom 25. und 26. Februar 2002 in Zusammenarbeit mit dem Europäischen Zentrum für Wohlfahrtspolitik und Sozialforschung. Wien.

Danzinger, A. and Kloimüller, I. (2001): Meisterhafte Pflegekunst. Gesundheitsgerechte Karrierewege im Pflegeberuf. Abschlussbericht PNr 160/IV/15. Älterwerden und Erfahrung in der Pflege – Bausteine für laterale und alter(n)sgerechte Karrieremodelle. Fonds gesundes Österreich. http://www.-fgoe.org/projektfoerderung/gefoerderte-projekte/FgoeProject_219540/753-814. Visited: Nov. 22, 2007.

Danzinger, A. and Kloimüller, I. (2003): Meisterhafte Pflegekunst – alter(n)sgerechte Karrierewege im Pflegeberuf. Abschlussbericht II für den Fonds Gesundes Österreich. Proj.Nr 529 /I/304. Wien.

Eberherr, H., Fleischmann, A. and Hoffmann, R. (2006): Alter(n)svielfalt im Betrieb. Strategien und Maßnahmen für eine nachhaltige Unternehmenspolitik in kleinen und mittleren Unternehmen. Arbeitsbereich Gender and Diversity in Organizations. Wien.. http://www.toolbox.elderly.at/attach/-guideline_alternsvielfalt_im_betrieb.pdf. Visited: Nov. 22, 2007.

Europäische Kommission (2007): Europa in Zahlen – Eurostat Jahrbuch 2006-07. Amt für amtliche Veröffentlichungen der Europäischen Gemeinschaften. Luxemburg. http://epp.eurostat.ec.europa.eu/cache/ITY_OFFPUB/KS-CD -06-001/DE/KS-CD-06-001-DE.PDF. Visited: Nov. 22, 2007.

ILO (2005): 7th ILO European Regional Meeting. http://www.ilo.org/global/ About_the_ILO/Media_and_public_information/Press_releases/lang-en/ WCMS_005181/index.htm. Visited: Dec. 21, 2007.

Ilmarinen, J. (1995): Arbeitsfähigkeit und Alter. In: Betriebliche Gesundheitsförderung für älterwerdende Arbeitnehmer (Karazman, R., Geißler, H., Kloimüller, I. and Winker, N. (eds.)). Conrad. Gamburg, 15–33.

Naegele, G. (1992): Zwischen Arbeit und Rente. Gesellschaftliche Chancen und Risken älterer Arbeitnehmer. Maro Verlag. Augsburg.

Rimser M. (2006): Generation Resource Management: Nachhaltige HR-Konzepte im demografischen Wandel. Rosenberger Fachverlag, Leonberg.

Statistik Austria (2007): http://www.statistik.at/web_de/statistiken/bevoelkerung/-volkszaehlungen/erwerbspersonen/023333.html. Visited: Dec. 21, 2007.

Weiler, A. (2005): European Foundation for the Improvement of Living and Working Conditions; annual review of working conditions in the EU: 2004-2005, Luxembourg Office for Official Publications of the European Communities. http://www.eurofound.europa.eu/ewco/reports/EU0502AR-01/EU0502AR01.pdf. Visited: Oct. 24, 2007.

Suggestions for Further Reading

Huuhtanen, P., Kalimo, R., Lindström, K., Linkola, P. and Liukkunen, U. (1992): Ageing workers and changing working life. Ministry of Labour. Finnish Institute of Occupational Health. Helsinki.

Ilmarinen, J. and Tempel, J. (2002): Arbeitsfähigkeit 2010. Was können wir tun, damit Sie gesund bleiben? VSA Verlag. Hamburg.

Karazman, R., Geissler, H., Kloimüller, I. and Winker, N. (1995): Betriebliche Gesundheitsförderung für älterwerdende Arbeitnehmer. Conrad. Gamburg.

Kriener, B., Neudorfer, E. and Künzel, D. (2004): Gesund durchs Arbeitsleben. Empfehlungen für eine zukunfts- und alternsorientierte betriebliche Gesundheitsförderung in Klein- und Mittelunternehmen. Wien. Wirtschaftskammer Österreich. http://wko.at/sp/bgf/BGFStudie.pdf. Visited: Nov. 22, 2007.

Mandl, I., Dorr, A. and Oberholzner, T. (2006): Age and Employment in the New Member States. European Foundation for the Improvement of Living and Working Conditions. Dublin. http://www.eurofound.europa.eu/pubdocs/-2006/26/en/1/ef0626en.pdf. Visited: Nov. 22, 2007.

Marilyn Clarke, Linley Hartmann and Margaret Patrickson

Factors Influencing Work or Retirement Decisions for Australian Women Academics

Introduction

In the early 2000s, what was previously a future scenario of workforce shortages of skilled workers and unsustainable pension demands has became an issue for today as the implications of growing numbers of older people who are reliant on government support and services is of concern to governments in Australia and other places (AG 2007). A higher proportion of the population is of retirement age and the growth of the working age population is slowing. Dealing with this issue is now a key policy development area in many countries. OECD individual country reports indicate that Australia has a number of issues to address including the strengthening of older workers' employability, preventing the use of disability pensions as a pathway to early retirement and increasing awareness of age discrimination legislation. Figure 1 (OECD 20005a) shows the relative position of Australia compared with other countries in the workforce participation of older workers in 1995 and 2003.

Predicted outcomes of these demographic changes include slower economic growth and further increases in public expenditure, particularly in the health sector (ABS 2006). Partly in consequence of these predictions governments are now urging older workers to remain in the workforce as long as possible, yet, at the same time, many are being encouraged by employers to leave long term career jobs (Encel 2003). Employers continue to stereotype older workers with regard to their ability to cope with the work, their capacity for change and their overall image in comparison to younger, seemingly more capable employees.

Yet the decision to work or retire is more complex than these comments would suggest. We propose that work and retirement options for older women in 2007 are influenced by a number of factors (financial circumstances in work and retirement; employment issues such as career history and present status; social and personal contexts such as family circumstances, health, and other interests) which differ in many aspects from those in past decades. Since integrating these variables to provide a snapshot of older women and their career or retirement options is a complex task, we have chosen to focus on one particular group, that of the older woman academic in the Australian university system. In dealing with this specific group we acknowledge that we are focusing on a middle socio-economic grouping yet this group provides some interesting insights into a range of issues that are also of relevance to older women from other career groups.

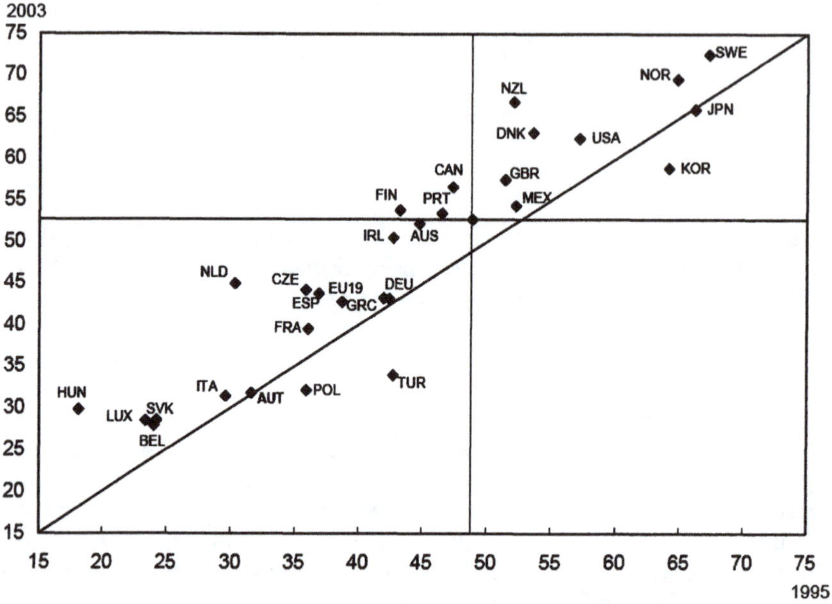

Figure 1: Participation rates (percentages) of 55-65 year old workers in OECD countries, 1995 and 2003 (OECD 2005b): Ageing and Employment Policies: Austria

In the first part we introduce our model of work and retirement options and influences. We then explain the Australian scenario by briefly providing some background on Australian population demographics, employment demand and opportunities particularly in the University sector. We review Australian legislation influencing retirement options through age pension provisions, removal of age discrimination, tax treatment and access to retirement savings. Some fundamentals of the financial provisions for retirement in Australia have changed dramatically since the 1990s with more changes projected for 2007, and recent developments in Europe point in a similar direction. We then illustrate our model by examining the situations older women academics find themselves in and look at the options available to them before we suggest some actions for universities and individuals.

Work/Retirement Options and Influences

Our research on men and women in late working life and early retirement has extended from the mid 1980s to the mid 1990s and it has been interesting for us to reflect on the changes that have occurred during that time. Our samples of men and women in private and public sector organizations provided us with a good basis for understanding the dynamics of end of working life decisions and this has been complemented by our own experiences with University life as we ourselves have reached older worker status.

From this research (Patrickson and Hartmann 1992, 1995, 1996a, 1996b; Patrickson, Hartmann and McCarron 1994) and our subsequent readings we have refined a model for discussion (see Figure 2).

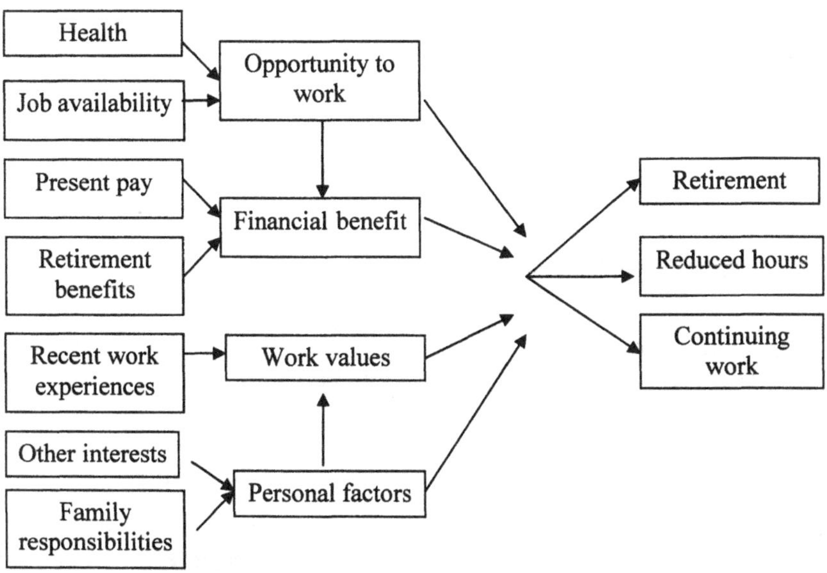

Figure 2: Work/Retirement options for older workers and the factors influencing take-up of these

We limit our definition of older women workers to those 55 years of age and older, as this is the age at which retirement savings can be accessed in Australia. Our model identifies three options for older women in the workforce – retirement, part-retirement/part-work, and continuing present work arrangements. Sometimes part-time work is a transition period before full retirement. We suggest four variables influence which of these outcomes occurs – opportunity to work which includes availability of jobs and health capacity to work; financial benefit which includes pay rates for continuing work and present and anticipated financial resources for retirement; work values which may be influenced by treatment as an older worker in the present work situation but also the importance of financial reward, recognition and sense of achievement for example; and personal factors such as the extent of other interests and requirements of family responsibilities to care for aged parents or disabled spouse or children. Rarely is this a completely 'free choice'. For such a situation to occur no constraints would be present and all options would be available. There would need to be available and desirable work opportunities; good health; financial benefit from continuing to work but also the financial capability to retire; a positive, present work situation; valued personal opportunities provided by paid work and also unpaid situations in the pursuit of interests or volunteering; and a level of family responsibilities that can be accommodated within work or retirement.

An alternative finding of our research was that some women wanted to continue part-time work in order to have time away from their husbands, who were retiring. (Patrickson and Hartmann 1996a, 1996b). The practical realities of financial, career and personal circumstances may mean this is a decision over which many women have little control and that limitations within these factors limit the direction of their lives.

This model provides the framework within which this paper progresses. Before examining how these variables might apply to women in academic positions at Australian Universities we turn now to the Australian context and briefly identify changes over the last 20 years in population demographics, the education, income and workforce participation circumstances of men and women aged 50-59 years within the context of changing labour force demand.

Changing Circumstances of Older Workers: 1980s – 2000+

At the start of the 21st century older workers have significantly improved health outcomes compared with their parents (ABS 2006). A major factor in the ageing of the Australian population has been decreases in death rates for both men and women. In 2004, the death rate for men aged 50-59 years was less than half the rate in 1981 and for women it was just over half that of men of the same age. At age 60 they could have an active life for another 20+ years (AG 2007). The circumstances of older workers aged 50-59 years in 2007 show other differences from previous generations, particularly for women. For example:

- They are better educated. The proportion of 50-59 year olds with a post-school qualification increased from 33% in 1984 to 52% in 2005.
- From 1984 to 2005 the proportion of 50-59 year old women with a bachelor degree or above as their highest non-school qualification increased by

more than five and a half times (from 3% to 17%). The proportion of men with this qualification increased by almost three times (from 7% to 20%).

- The workforce participation of women aged 50-59 increased from 37% in 1984 to 62% in 2004, with about 40% working part time. Men's participation decreased slightly from 83% to 80% and men working part-time increased from 4% in 1984 to 10% in 2004. By age 59, part-time employment increases to a top rate of 17% for men and 39% for women.
- Over these 20 years the number of women aged 50-59 whose principal source of income was employment earnings increased from just over one third in 1982 (35%) to over half in 2003-04 (53%). The proportion of men aged 50-59 whose principal source of income was employment earnings decreased from 80% in 1982 to 70% in 2003-04.
- In that time, the proportion of 50-59 year olds not-in-the-labour force with private pensions as their principal source of household income doubled from 4% in 1982 to 8% in 2003-04. This means that 92% of those not-in-the-labour force relied on other income, spouse support or some government payments for their principle source of income.
- The following table shows how these trends extend to age 65, the government pension retirement age.

Categories of Participation	*1995*	*2000*	*2005*
% Total of Men in any employment	61.4%	60.7%	65.3%
% of Men employed part-time	13.5%	13.9%	16.4%
% Total of Women in any employment	27.9%	34.5%	43.8%
% of Women employed part-time	50.8%	51.3%	50.1%

Table 1: Employment rates in transition to retirement age: 55-64 years (ABS 2006)

Labour Force Demand

The industrial basis of the Australian labour market has changed considerably since the late 1980s. There has been a general decrease in employment in the goods-producing industries and an increase in service industries. Table 2 shows the main sources of employment for older men and women.

Industries x sex	1984 - %	2004 - %	Change
Men: 50-59 years			
Manufacturing	21.1	15.2	↓↓
Construction	8.2	11.6	↑
Property & Business Services	5.0	11.5	↑↑
Retail Trade	8.0	8.9	↑
Transport & Storage	8.1	7.7	↓
Women: 50-59 years			
Health & Community Services	17.9	23.0	↑↑
Education	13.9	16.0	↑
Retail	15.2	11.5	↓↓
Property & Business Services	6.8	10.5	↑
Manufacturing	12.2	7.1	↓↓

Table 2: Differences in employment in selected industries for employed males and females aged 50-59 years: 1984 and 2004 (ABS 2006)

Overall employment demand in health and community services, property and business services and education services provides increasing numbers of professional and semi-professional employment opportunities for women and in 2004 just over one third of the total female workforce was employed there. However, the Australian Bureau of Statistics noted that

> Greater proportions of women now have higher education qualifications.... However, it is women who continue to carry the greater responsibility for caring and other unpaid work, effectively placing them under increased time pressures. Women's working patterns may impact on their ability to balance work with other responsibilities. (ABS 2006)

Legislation Influencing Retirement Options

In Australia, in the majority of employment situations, there is no longer a compulsory retirement age. If people are to retire voluntarily they must have the financial means to do so and, as in the past, it is likely that financial incentives will continue to be used to 'encourage' unwanted older workers to leave long term employment. A key difference between Australia and many other countries is that taxpayers make no specific payments toward a government age pension and this pension is not an automatic entitlement on reaching pensionable age. Eligibility is means tested on the basis of income and assets. To reduce access to this government provided age pension and to provide better retirement income, private saving for retirement has been encouraged by all Australian political parties and has received a variety of taxation advantages for many years.

Private, non-government funded retirement pensions, called Superannuation, include many tax benefits and are accessible at age 55. The operation of Superannuation is complex with two major categories in operation.

The oldest category of private savings for retirement (and now becoming less common) includes funds linked to past employment through contributions to an employer or industry based pension fund. Prior to the 1990s, employees in public/government sector organizations with superannuation benefits had the choice of taking a life time pension, the amount of which was based on their final salary and length of service, or converting these funds to a 'lump sum' and investing it themselves. Only older employees with long term employment in Universities would most likely be in such a scheme.

Employees in private sector organizations usually received only a 'lump sum'. For white collar or 'salaried' employees, these payments could be accessed from age 55 with benefits increasing to age 65 although age 58-60 was usually the most financially advantageous time to retire as benefits increased at a lesser rate after this age. Many weekly paid or 'blue collar' employees were provided with less favourable or no retirement benefits. Those who changed employer generally lost most employer superannuation benefits on each change, a factor which discouraged job change especially in later employment years. At retirement, people could use their lump sum money to pay off debts, holiday and support themselves until they were 65, when they could qualify to receive an age pension. In salaried work, with a good employer retirement fund, a health problem increased the opportunity for a well funded, early retirement. Since the 1980s, redundancy with an extra 'early' retirement benefit (which received taxation concessions) has been a means for employers to downsize and in particular to 'retire' older workers.

As shown by statistics presented earlier in this paper, the death rate for older workers is now half that of 20 years ago. For life-time pension funds and government funded age pensions, this shorter life expectancy was a financial advantage. Life expectancy is now 80+ years for men and women and life time pension funds need to provide pensions for longer. Individuals also need to make their retirement savings last longer.

Since the early 1990s, the second major category of private retirement saving has been expanded and regulated by legislation which has enabled the development of retirement financial services providing a variety of types of investment based funds which are mostly independent of employers and of job changes and the payout from these funds is dependent upon investment gains. The government has initiated varied taxation regimes to encourage investment in "superannuation" by men and women of all age groups, particularly those over 40 years of age. These investments are usually property or share market related so Australians now have a greater involvement in private sector investment than at any other time in our history. They invest in and share the profits arising from downsizing and changes in work conditions. Rising share market values and also property values have increased with wealth of Australians and in particular, because of special taxation treatments, of Australians with superannuation.

In an article assessing the lessons of the Australian Superannuation System for the USA, Mitchell and O'Quinn (1997) identified the distinguishing features to be that workers contribute a set percentage (9% by from 2002) of their income through their employer to private savings plans and that this is augmented by tax-favoured voluntary contributions. At retirement, therefore, the intention is that workers should be able to draw a secure and comfortable annual income that at least matches the income they would receive under the original government age pension. They concluded that by 1997 this scheme was showing signs of success and significantly reduced long-term government budget pressures.

Retirement Wealth

Government pensions are the main source of income for older Australians and less than one third of retired Australians have received or currently receive some form of private superannuation income (ABS 2000).

In the total population, although similar percentages of men and women (about 72%) have some superannuation savings (that is private pension savings), the median value for females was half that of males, often because of their part-time employment and breaks in employment. Double income couples in which both had superannuation had a median balance 3.5 times greater than single income and superannuation couples (ABS 2000).

It is clear that those who have retired on superannuation rather than government age pension receive more income. The maximum age pension payment to an individual is about AUS$13,000 (€7,000) per annum and AUS$20,200 (€10,000) to couples. Almost half (45%) of those who took their superannuation as a lump sum received more than $20,000 (€12,000) per annum (ABS 2000).

The Choices Facing Older Workers

These financial boundaries are a major limiting determinant of the choices older workers are faced with since they determine their standard of living in retirement. Other major determinants are the extent to which current employment remains open or acceptable alternatives arise, work capacity in terms of health, and whether or not working helps fulfil personal values and enhances self esteem. We have already cited data which indicates that professionals, including education professionals have continuing high employment demand and hence should be more likely to find themselves with more open choices in their late working years. This group, with particular reference to the university sector, is the focus of this paper for several reasons. First it is a sector where employment choice is more open than many other areas. Second, in recent years there has been strong growth in female employment and consequently a high proportion of older women. Thirdly it is an area in which the three authors have personal experience as older female employees.

Older Women Academics in Universities – Employment, Finance, Work Values, Personal Variables

During the 1990s, Australian tertiary education needed to supplement reduced government funding and chose to do so by providing services both within Australia and off-shore to growing numbers of international students, mainly from Asia. During this period the proportion of women students increased to approximately half the total and their primary study areas were the non-traditional sciences including business, health education, and social sciences. By 2002, stark gender differences strengthened in fields of study. More than three-quarters of all undergraduate students studying in the fields of education and health in 2002 were female. By contrast, 85% of students enrolled in undergraduate engineering and related degrees, and over 75% of those in information technology degrees, were men (Carrington and Pratt 2003).

An Australian Vice-Chancellor's Committee Report (2005) reviewing barriers to the promotion of women academics indicated that between 1996 and 2004 there was an almost uninterrupted increase in the number of women academics at all academic levels. In the disciplines of commerce, management and health, where the growth of female students was significant, more women were also appointed as teaching staff. Yet these disciplines did not have a long history of academic study in universities and so there was not a tradition of study at post-graduate level, e.g. PhD, and few women had this qualification.

In 1994, of 32,000 staff in Australian Universities, 33% were women as were 12% of Associate Professors and Professors. In 2004, staff had increased to 35,000 of whom 39% were women who comprised 16% of Professors, 24% of Associate Professors, and 35% of Senior Lectures. In 2000-2002 women had lower success in applying for promotion than did men for all the senior academic positions – that is Professor, Associate Professor, and Senior Lecturer.

Within this period the University context has dramatically changed. It has now become essential for all academics to obtain PhD qualifications in research, to publish in top ranking journals, and to be visible in contributing to professional debate within one's field of expertise. Whereas twenty years ago, an academic caeer was marked by flexibility in work scheduling which allowed time for working at home, consulting work, and pursuit of academic interests, this traditional flexibility and potential work-life balance has been undermined by increasing workloads and the change from traditional University to 'teaching factory' (Doherty and Manfredi 2006).

Today, the tasks of building teaching income, pursuit of research outcomes and successful grant applications, and supervision of successful PhD students are likely to dominate work schedules. White (2001) concludes that the increasing globalisation of higher education has redefined the role of the academic to be entrepreneur and manager.

For Australian Universities the median age of academics is 48 years: 20% aged 50-54; 25% aged 55+, that is of potential retirement age (up from 22% in 2002); and 2.6% are over 65 (Unisa 2005). Replacing them will not be easy as the same situation applies globally and academic salaries are less than competitive with similar professional earnings (Macnamara 2006). Anecdotal evidence suggests that a two tier system of employment is emerging – high compensation for high profile academics and lower compensation for the remainder. "Academic stars" (Doherty and Manfredi 2006) who obtain grants and publish are in high demand. Within the Australian industrial relations system, Workplace Agreements include the option of individual contracts which mean that attractive conditions of employment can be freely negotiated for "academic stars" but there are fewer options and choices for other staff.

The circumstances under which older academics are now employed are therefore different from those at entry and perhaps, what many women would have valued. In particular, the previous data on promotion indicates that more men were successful in their aspirations for promotion during the last decade. White (2001) argues that this continuing imbalance reflects an emphasis on research as the main criteria for promotion, new managerialism, globalisation and the redefinition of the role of academics. Even if one acquires the right qualifications later in career, it is difficult to achieve sufficient research impetus in a short time to qualify for promotion to associate or full professor.

Many older staff in the booming study areas do not fit the profile required for a successful academic career (White 2001; Doherty and Manfredi 2006). They do not have the qualifications and research portfolios that are linked to excellence in research and teaching and more importantly, to the obtaining of research grants and publications which determine University funding and status. Late entry, lower qualifications, career breaks and post PhD research based promotion criteria penalized older women in particular such that they were less likely to meet promotion criteria and hence were earning less income and had less superannuation accumulated. Changing work demands and the differently defined outputs have halted the career progression for many middle and late career female staff who are least able to afford to retire. This may not be such an issue for a minority for whom research and teaching have been an integral part of their careers. These women are also likely to be advantaged financially by having had fewer or no career breaks and promotion which has brought better superannuation, and a higher general level of saving. Nevertheless, they too may experience some dissatisfaction as they witness the employment of high profile "academic stars" (Doherty and Manfredi 2006) on lucrative individual work contracts.

The authors of this paper have developed a table summarizing these points and illustrating the contrast between these two groups of academic women as they approach their late working life (see Figure 3).

The situation of older female academics contemplating retirement falls into two main categories. Those who have obtained a PhD, are research active, have had a relatively unbroken academic career, have been able to accumulate adequate levels of superannuation, are in good health and are not under pressure from family responsibilities, have a range of options and choices with regards to when they will retire and whether or not retirement will mean the end to paid employment.

However, many women trying to juggle work and family have experienced a different career path. They have often had broken periods of service which have impacted in terms of career achievements including promotions, research activities, the completion of a higher degree and the capacity to network within their discipline.

The impact has also been felt in terms of finances – the women at the lower end of the academic scale are the ones most likely to have had periods of unemployment or underemployment and thus to have accumulated less in superannuation benefits and other assets. Their later work life is likely to be characterized by heavy teaching and administrative loads so that even those who are in good health may find that the pressure and stress of the job is becoming untenable. For women in this group the choices and options are much less attractive: to remain in a highly pressured job or to retire with inadequate superannuation to fund a reasonable lifestyle.

Given the high proportion of Australian academics who are older and therefore likely to leave the paid workforce within the next decade, the way in which these exits are managed will become a critical issue for universities as well as for the national economy. We suggest there are two perspectives from which this can be addressed – university and individuals.

	Group 1 Completed PhD and managed research and teaching components within their careers Fairly continuous career	Group 2 Involved mainly in teaching and obtained higher research qualifications late or not at all Late entry or broken career progression
Opportunity to work	Tenured with opportunity for part time contract for one year and further casual work after retirement at lower pay Or Emeritus appointment Health may be a consideration	Probably tenured or at least fixed term contract with opportunity for part time contract for one year and further casual work after retirement at lower pay Or Adjunct appointment Health a consideration
Financial benefit	Contributed to superannuation (which was voluntary until 1990) for a long time so should be satisfactory for retirement Therefore casual and part time work not of much benefit	Late contribution to superannuation – may be inadequate Therefore tries to remain working and exploit extra teaching opportunities
Work values	Present work situation demanding but has high status in organization that assists with survival Under increasing pressure to develop media and business skills beyond academic interests	Present work situation demanding and because of lack of promotion opportunities feels unappreciated and exploited Under pressure to perform at a higher academic level or increase low level work load
Personal factors	Research interests integrated with other life interests Academic flexibility may have assisted family-work life balance New demands from aged/disabled parents, partner, children Less conflict so better general health	Long term studying for PhD and working and balancing family demands with little time for developing own interests Maybe new demands from aged/disabled parents, partner, children On-going stress may have affected general health

Figure 3: Career paths and outcomes for women academics in late career

Options for University Employers

Earlier in this paper we have reviewed the change in emphasis in staffing appointments from teaching to research. However, if too many of the older 'teaching' staff retire, this will put the new cohort of research oriented appointees under pressure to teach and perhaps diminish their research outcomes. Universities are therefore in a 'tricky' situation.

The University of South Australia (Unisa 2005) emphasizes the need to capture the knowledge of older staff whilst at the same time encouraging them to retire, either specifically to make way for younger staff or because their skills and knowledge are seen as outdated. The University argues that short term actions focusing on employing and retaining retirement-age workers through flexible work arrangements, salary/benefit incentives and developmental opportunities, as well as practices to assist the transition of staff to retirement need to be balanced with long term action to replace the skills, knowledge and capabilities that may be lost from the workforce. Yet until recently special incentives in the period leading up to retirement were offered in return for agreeing to specified retirement dates. This strategy aids in workforce planning as well as in encouraging the retirement of older academics that are no longer valued within the new managerial system. Another renewal strategy adopted by many universities in Australia and elsewhere is to attract foreign PhD students with a view to recruiting them to academic positions upon graduation. (Macnamara 2006)

For universities, the option of phased retirement would seem to benefit both universities and academics. Universities would be better able to manage the transfer of knowledge, for example through mentoring programs, as well as having a clearer picture of retirement intentions which would contribute to workforce planning processes. Staff would benefit through a more gradual transition to retirement, allowing time for both psychological and financial adjustments. Those with inadequate retirement savings would have the opportunity to continue contributing to superannuation but not have to continue working under the same workload pressures. Phased retirement programs have the potential to meet the needs of both highly successful women researchers and those whose careers have been hampered by a range of personal and career constraints. They would be particularly beneficial to women with family responsibilities such as care of an elderly parent, care of grandchildren or care of a sick or disabled spouse.

A second option is to nurture valued staff who do retire not just by providing them with emeritus status and small amounts of paid work supervising, teaching or researching but by nurturing their involvement with other academics in on-going intellectual involvement in university work, for example, as mentors, and as 'wild card' researchers, or as 'research helpers' thereby increasing university resources. It is not enough to provide office space and leave them alone. Retirees will want differing levels of responsibility and flexibility to maintain their interest relative to other retirement temptations and therefore need appropriate management if they are to retain their involvement.

Options for Older Women Academics

From the foregoing analysis, it would seem that the late working life options of older women academics are very much influenced by the development of their careers, in particular timing of entry to university life, timing of gaining doctoral qualifications, and ability to sustain effort toward publications. Group 1 is better positioned to receive valued and better work options, given their early doctoral attainment and early entry into university employment, which has provided flexible opportunities to suit them. Group 2 is less likely to be valued or have flexible work options available to them, given their late entry and late attainment of their qualifications and thus they are in a less powerful position with respect to the university that employs them. In terms of retirement options, Group 1 is likely to be better financially prepared and their career status has enabled them to generate stronger sources of income based assets such that they are therefore in a stronger position to pursue other interests if they so desire. Group 2 is likely to be less financially secure; experience more stress and lower recognition and have less flexibility in accommodating personal pressures and pursuing other interests.

Women academics would benefit from developing both a short term and long term strategic view of their late working life options. If women academics want stressful lives undertaking on-demand work with less flexibility and potentially lower relative pay and reduced late-working life options then they are faced with the outcomes of such options which include undertaking tasks (teaching) in which they are easily replaced as they become older, and consequently face exhaustion trying to meet family and career demands. If women academics want well rewarded, flexible, late work life options they need to position themselves to offer unique and valued competencies to their universities. This may require a long term plan plus strategic and lateral thinking; a re-thinking of their values and priorities; and development of new cognitive maps to reduce conflicts in priorities and satisfy work and non-work demands.

Conclusion

In this paper we have attempted to examine the factors which influence work or retirement choices for older women academic staff in Australia by first examining our model of these factors, secondly by identifying key features of the Australian and particular university context and thirdly identifying two general streams of life experiences that may assist in understanding the context of the circumstances of older women academics. We have then made some suggestions for individuals and university. From our analysis it becomes clear that both finances and career circumstances are the essential factors within which the influence of other factors are played out. More importantly, all these factors are shaped over an extended period, together. Women who want to have good work/retirement options need to be alert to the factors leading to these from an early age and maintain both career and family orientations. It also seems clear, that with their new business orientation, Universities have not yet fully understood the potential of their retired staff to enjoy voluntary work that is intellectually interesting within a range of potential responsibilities.

Literature

Academy of the Social Sciences in Australia (2004): Australian Women Facing the Future: Is the Intergenerational Report Gender-neutral? An Academy sponsored workshop held in Brisbane, 1-2 July 2004.

Anderson, G. (2006): Carving out Time and Space in the Managerial University. Journal of Organizational Change Management, 19/5: 578-592.

ABS - Australian Bureau of Statistics (2006): Australian Social Trends Cat. no. 4102.0 ABS, Canberra. http://www.abs.gov.au/ausstats/abs@.nsf/Latest-products/C36BD992C71C3343CA2571B0000EA934?opendocument. Visited: 27 July 2006.

ABS - Australian Bureau of Statistics (2000): 6360.0 - Superannuation: Coverage and Financial Characteristics, ABS Canberra. http://www.abs.gov.au/Aus-stats/abs@.nsf/Latestproducts/6360.0Main%20Features1Jun%202000?o-pendocument&tabname=Summary&prodno=6360.0&issue=Jun%202000 &num=&view. Visited: 27 July 2006.

AG - Australian Government (2007): Intergenerational Report – 2007. http://-www.treasury.gov.au/igr. Visited: 14 April 2007.

AVCC - Australian Vice-Chancellors Committee (2005): National Colloquium of Senior Women in Higher Education. The great barrier myth: and investigation of promotions policy and practice. University of SA. http://www.-avcc.edu.au/documents/policies_programs/women/FinalAVCCReportJuly-05.pdf. Visited: 27 July 2006.

AVCC - Australian Vice Chancellor's Committee (2006): The Second Action Plan for Women Employed in Australian Universities 2006-2010. http://-www.avcc.edu.au/documents/policies_programs/women/AVCC-Action-Plan-for-Women-2006.pdf. Visited: 27 July 2006.

Carrington, K. and Pratt, A. (2003): How Far Have We Come? Gender Disparities in the Australian Higher Education System. Department of the Parliamentary Library, Canberra, Australia. http://www.avcc.edu.au/documents/policiesprograms/women/Gender_Disparities_20Report_Jun03. Visited: 15 September 2006.

Doherty, L. and Manfredi, S. (2006): Action Research to Develop Work-life Balance in a UK University. Women in Management Review, 21/3: 241-259.

Encel, S. (2003): Age Can Work: The case for older Australians staying in the workforce. A report prepared for the Australian Council of Trade Unions and the Business Council of Australia. Social Policy Research Centre, University of NSW.

Granleese, J. and Sayer, G. (2006): Gendered Ageism and 'Lookism' a Triple Jeopardy for Female Academics. Women in Management Review, 21/6: 500-517.

Kryger, T. (2004): Australia's Ageing Workforce. Research Note Information, Analysis and Advice for the Parliament 7 March 2005, no. 35: 2004–05. Parliament of Australia Department of Parliamentary Services. Parliamentary Library ISSN 1449-8456.

Macnamara, L. (2006): Academic Shortage Looms. The Australia, May 31:29.

Mitchell, D.J. and O'Quinn, R.P. (1997): Australia's Privatized Retirement System: Lessons for the United States. Retirement Income and Security. http://www.heritage.org/Research/SocialSecurity/BG1149.cfm. Visited: 15 September 2006.

OECD (2005a): Ageing and Employment Policies: Australia. http://www.oecd.-org/dataoecd/61/4/38107362.pdf. Visited: 15 February 2007.

OECD (2005b): Ageing and Employment Policies: Austria. http://www.oecd.org/-document/60/0,2340,en_2649_37435_35283132_1_1_1_37435,00.html. Visited: 15 February 2007.

Patrickson, M.G., Hartmann, L.C. and McCarron, L. (1994): Women in Education and Early Retirement. Journal of Educational Administration, 32/4:77-85.

Patrickson, M.G. and Hartmann, L.C. (2001): Human Resource Management in Australia: Prospects for the Twenty-first Century. International Journal of Manpower, vol. 22, no. 3:198-206.

Patrickson, M.G. and Hartmann, L.C. (1992): Workforce Participation Choices of Older Males. Asia Pacific Journal of Human Resources, vol. 30, no. 3, Spring 1992, 40-48.

Patrickson, M.G. and Hartmann, L.C. (1995): Australia's Ageing Population: Implications for Human Resource Management. International Journal of Manpower, vol. 16, no. 5/6, 34-46.

Patrickson, M.G. and Hartmann, L.C. (1996a): Australian Gender Differences in Preferences for Early Retirement. International Employment Relations Review, vol. 2, no. 1, 1-19.

Patrickson, M.G. and Hartmann, L.C. (1996b): Older Women: Retailing utilizes a neglected workforce resource. Asia Pacific Journal of Human Resources, vol. 34, no. 2: 88-98.

Sheen, V, (2002): Older Women in Australia's Workforce. How are older women faring in Australia's ageing workforce? Presentation to Australian Women Speak Inaugural National Women's Conference. Office of the Status of Women National Convention Centre. Canberra, 26-28 August 2001: Australian Council of the Ageing.

Schofield, D.J. and Beard, J.R., (2005): Baby Boomer Doctors and Nurses: Demographic Change and Transitions to Retirement. MJA, 183/2: 80-83.

Thanacoody, P.R., Bartram, T., Barker, M. and Jacobs, K. (2006): Career Progression among Female Academics: A Comparative Study of Australia and Mauritius. Women in Management Review, 21/7: 536-553.

Unisa (2005): Annual Report 2004/5 University of South Australia.

White, K. (2001): Women in the Professoriate in Australia. International Journal of Organisational Behaviour, 3/2: 64-76.

Williams, N. (2006): Over-60s Staying in the Workforce. The Advertiser 'Career One', Feb 10.

Linley Hartmann and Helene Mayerhofer

Career Opportunities for Older Women: Does Career Capital Theory Assist in Understanding the Options they Have?

What does the term "old" mean in the context of the labour market? The answer seems to be: 40 years for women and 45 for men. Career stages and career opportunities are connected to a person's stage of life, even if human resource managers and others who decide about an employee's promotion reject this notion. Like his or her sex, a person's age can be seen and it obviously is a relevant feature which has to be taken into account when it comes to employment. You can be too young but also too old to fit into a specific career stage or into a specific position. At least in Europe, seniority no longer seems a widely accepted distribution principle as far as salaries and career positions are concerned. This has changed the situation for young people on the labour market. Nowadays, one can even find full professors at University who are not older than 30 years of age. Apparently, being very young can sometimes mean being very successful. However, what does age mean in terms of career opportunities of older employees, and of older women in particular?

In this paper, it is not our purpose to review all career concepts or all the ways in which career capital can be defined, but rather to examine one definition of career capital as a career management tool as well as the so-called protean and boundaryless career theories in which this tool has been developed. We address the following question: Can the concept of career capital assist women in managing their late working lives across a broad spectrum of employment situations? In order to examine this question, we considered the changing work and retirement parameters faced by older women as well as the similarities and differences in the situations women encounter in two seemingly similar economies – those of Austria and Australia. We conclude that factors influencing the options presented to women in each economy differ considerably, but we also show that there are potential similarities which make the concept of career capital increasingly relevant in both countries.

Introduction

Careers may be defined as paths involving a sequence of job opportunities (the term "job" is used in its broad definition here) that go beyond a single employment setting and involve adapting to changing circumstances (Defillippi and Arthur 1994). More significantly, career can be seen as a major part of life, especially when it is considered to provide not just a regular income but also a sense of purpose, a challenge, self-fulfilment, status, and social contacts. Careers can be considered as journeys through life. The interpretation of whether career steps are defined by individuals or by organisations has varied over the last few decades (Baruch 2004). In early human resource management literature, career management was often identified as an organisational function rather than an activity undertaken by individuals to enhance their career opportunities. HRM practices, such as strategic HRM, consider career management as a system within the organisation and assume responsibility for this in a variety of ways (Baruch and Peiperl 2000).

The widespread acceptance of new career concepts, such as the boundaryless career and the *protean* career, as "accepted metaphors in the field of career theory" (Briscoe and Hall 2006a:4), have highlighted a shift in the thinking of some organisations and individuals. Baruch and Peiperl (2000) note that such career concepts focus on the individual without giving sufficient recognition to the links between organisations and individuals, which, however, continue to play a vital role, even though they may be less permanent than they used to be in the context of traditional long-term organisational careers. Organisations which have skilled yet transient employees benefit if these employees manage their careers successfully and may develop career management activities to foster career management, if only to ensure that the organisation's labour requirements can be met. Without a long-term psychological contract, it cannot be assumed that long-term employees will focus on career investment in one organisation (Mayrhofer et al. 2005; Hauff 2007). Individuals may seek to fulfil their interests and maximise their financial returns by career management actions that enhance their options. For example, individuals may select developmental and strategic activities that involve knowledge, skills, and abilities which are in high demand on the labour market and which are of interest to them. As a result, they might benefit by having better and more varied options, as well as by receiving personal and financial rewards. We will begin this paper by examining the most recent findings on the relevance of the new career concepts mentioned above and revisit the model of Sonnenfeld and Peiperl (1988), since it provides evidence that employment contracts have always been varied depending on business/organisational needs. We will then assess the extent to which even employees in fairly conventional forms of employment may benefit from taking a career management approach that focuses on building career competence or career capital.

In the next section we will compare older women's working lives in two countries with similar names but many differences in their economic and political frameworks – Austria and Australia. With regard to the Austrian labour market, it should be noted that the expansion of the European Union and the opening of

Eastern European countries to economic involvement by Austrian companies have provided a powerful impetus for expansion and, in some cases, for relocation of existing businesses, as well as for the development of new businesses in Austria. Concurrently, the arrival of many semi-skilled and unskilled people from Eastern countries has created new social and political challenges for the Austrian government. These changes, the privatisation of former government services, (for example, the national railway, telecom, and post), and the deregulation of business and employment conditions have changed life in Austria. The expansion of shopping hours is just one example of changes which have had an effect on the organisation of work as well as on family life. Interestingly, similar changes have occurred in Australia. There, changes have taken place in a different context, for instance, with regard to controlled migration or the business and mining resources boom, which, in turn, has brought unemployment to low levels. Recent governments, including the conservative government (from 1996 to 2007), have legislated major changes affecting business, government, employment relationships, and the power of unions. The impact recent changes regarding the government will have on society remains unclear. In both countries, the directions taken are similar but, as will be explained, there are fundamental differences in their approaches to social security, which makes it even more interesting to compare the two countries.

We will make an attempt to assess how the changes mentioned above influence women's late working life options. The rising generation of older women in the workforce is likely to face more favourable labour market conditions than in the past, as skill shortages are becoming evident in many countries and, at the same time, government-funded retirement incomes are under increasing pressure as populations age. Will the changes regarding labour market conditions lead to better chances and possibilities for older woman to get the highly valued positions they want? What are the career positions they would like to occupy? To reflect on the differences between organisational and individual career concepts, we will analyse the permanently changing definition of the term *career*.

Careers and Career Theory

In their review of prevailing career theories in the last two decades of the 20th century, Baruch and Peiperl (2000) argue that most theoretical models of career management tend to focus on individual rather than on organisational perspectives. This also holds true for two career concepts that have been developed to fit changes in employment relationships: the boundaryless career and the *protean* career.

The notion of a boundaryless career incorporates people's movements across organisations by focussing on physically boundaryless careers with an enhanced occupational or professional emphasis rather than on long-term employment with one organisation. It also stresses the accompanying psychological aspect that involves the capacity to make transitions. Arthur and Rousseau (1996) identified six examples of boundaryless careers represented by (1) high technology careers and movement across organisations; (2) by academics drawing validation from outside their present employment; (3) by real estate agents sustained by external networks; (4) by those individuals rejecting traditional assumptions of hierarchy and advancement; (5) by those incorporating family or personal priorities; and (6) by individuals perceiving themselves as boundaryless. All these options incorporate the notion of self-directed and values-driven career management undertaken by the individual.

Briscoe and Hall (2006a) define a protean career as self-directed and independent career behaviour, based on individually defined goals, encompassing the whole life-space, and driven by psychological rather than objective success, such as pay, rank, or power. In other words, such careers are influenced by the individual's set of values and are self-directed by individuals, as they adapt to circumstances that influence their performance as well as to the learning demands arising from their careers. A person in a boundaryless career is likely to act in a protean fashion. A protean career is a mindset that claims freedom, self-direction, and choices based on personal values. Ultimately, it is the perception of the individual which counts and, therefore, single organisation (in other words *bounded*) careers may be protean, if individuals believe that they have a certain degree of self-direction, independence, and a work-life-balance related to their values. Hence, boundaryless and protean careers are related but, nonetheless, independent constructs (Briscoe and Hall 2006a). In both conceptions, the value component within the theory is defined as a rejection of hierarchy and advancement, pay, rank, and power. To examine whether these values were widely adopted and whether they were a result of a lack of advancement possibilities or of changing values regarding career commitment and work-life-balance, would go beyond the scope of this paper. However, in 2008, higher salaries, rank, and power still seem to be important components in creating further career opportunities, components that can assist in creating the freedom for psychological success as well as the flexibility desired by individuals in categories 4 to 6 above.

The base from which the new career ideas originally developed becomes clearer when considering Sonnenfeld and Peiperl's (1988) typology of career systems. This classification was based on the entry, development, and exit strategies that distinguished the management practices of different U.S. firms and, ultimately, on their reliance on internal versus external labour markets. They identify two main characteristics of career systems within organisations: supply flow - movement in and out of the organisation - and internal movement or assignment, which is the flow across job assignments and promotions (see Figure 1). 20-year-old concepts like this indicate the range of employment circumstances then available in the U.S.A. and provide an interesting basis for contemporary investigations.

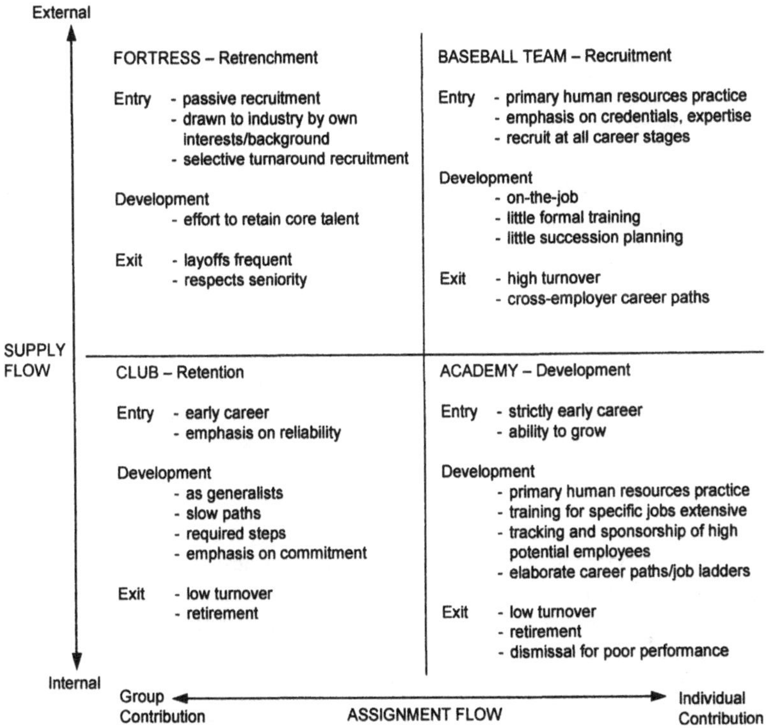

Figure 1: Model of career systems (Sonnenfeld and Peiperl 1988: 591)

Sonnenfeld and Peiperl (1988) identified typical industries for each model (see Figure 1). The Fortress model was linked to hotel (contemporary tourism providers), retail, publishing, textile, and natural resources industries and is characterised by the organisation's focus on survival and by a low commitment to individuals. The Baseball team model was linked to broadcasting, entertainment, bio-research, software development, investment banks, law firms, consulting firms, and public relations, and the metaphorical title was chosen because sports teams rely on skilled individual performers as well as on an open external labour market managed by agents and talent scouts. The Club model was linked to utilities, museums, government agencies, defence, airlines, and banks, where internal labour supply is developed and group factors are important. The Academy model was linked to automobile, electronic, pharmaceutical, office product, and consumer product industries, which are stable and strive to develop their employees' knowledge skills and commitment. With respect to possible exit strategies, the Fortress system respects seniority, but only the Club and the Academy systems mention retirement as a way out of the organisation.

Sonnenfeld and Peiperl's twenty-year-old system is one of the few practical representations of different employment systems and illustrates the widespread use of different employment contracts prior to the High Technology revolution, which prompted the development of the protean and boundaryless career concepts. Yet, it fails to include an increasingly relevant aspect which contemporary systems are able to account for: the side-by-side presence of a casual/temporary labour component in addition to a permanent/contractual workforce.

The expansion of boundaryless careers was attributed to the development of new forms of organisation in new technology companies, but the systems shown above indicate their relevance for other industries, including community, health, and education services, where many women are employed. It is not difficult to transpose the career circumstances that Defillippi and Arthur (1994) considered applicable to rapidly developing technological firms to the sectors mentioned above. In higher education, people with teaching competencies in particular fields may obtain teaching contracts in a range of educational institutions; the positions academics occupy involve a range of responsibilities – research, administration, and teaching – and moving from one focus to the other does not result in a loss of status (Baruch 2004). In health services, the skills of highly trained therapists or medical specialists may be shared across a number of locations, and their career success may depend on their reputation as well as on the degree of their involvement with a number of different organisations. A specialist service provider needs to network in order to know where her services are required, why she is to be involved rather than on-site staff, and how to engage in and contribute to a given situation. In order for local staff to gain access to specialist staff, their required competencies may include a clear understanding of the internal or external resourcing strategies of their organisation, specific skills in recognizing how particular clients can be assisted, and the knowledge of who has the skills to provide these services and of how to involve them.

Even before Defillippi and Arthur (1994) described the features of boundaryless career systems, structures like the ones they mention were common within organisations or as internal/external interfaces in service organisations. The way in which contemporary work environments differ from such earlier structures is that specialist service providers or consultants are more likely to be self-employed or to work for a consulting enterprise rather than in the user organisation. Mayrhofer et al (2005: 252) refer to these people as "free floating professionals". In HRM, practitioners with competencies and interests in particular fields, for example training, often work self-employed or from consulting businesses that provide specific services to a range of organisations rather than from training departments within large organisations. This development has certain parallels with the new forms of intra-firm relationship and starburst organisation associated with the introduction of new technologies in engineering and production in the late 1900s.

Much of the research on this topic has been based on experiences in the U.S.A., but, as will be shown at a later point, similar situations are identifiable in Austria and Australia. More recent research is attempting to clarify what career expectations employees have and how employers can manage employment relationships successfully (Roehling et al. 2000) and to develop models which reveal the typologies of different types of careers. Sullivan and Arthur (2006), for example, argue that attitudes to a boundaryless career can be characterised by varying levels of physical (objective) and psychological (subjective) mobility. The positions they describe are: (1) dependence due to an inability to define priorities or to behaviourally manage one's own career; (2) reaction because values are unclear and do not provide a perspective to guide decisions; (3) rigidity when values are known but the individual is not able to adapt performance and learning requirements and in such a way shape their career; and (4) protean management incorporating self-direction in line with values. In this investigation, preferences for mobility were not necessarily associated with other attributes of self-direction and of values-driven career management. Hence, it is suggested that this new way of viewing career determination may be applicable to a range of career settings and is a worthwhile concept in itself. There is, however, a big gap between identifying self-direction in line with personal values as a career management strategy and understanding the successful use of this strategy in a range of employment settings. In this regard, the concept of career competencies or career capital proves extremely useful.

The Concept of Career Capital

Career capital, human capital, or career competence are often interchangeable terms that assist in conveying the idea of individuals possessing valuable skills, knowledge, and abilities which they bring to their work and build throughout a life-time career (Defillippi and Arthur 1994; Dickman and Harris 2005). A resource base view of organisational competence would define these capacities as firm-specific or generic. An individual whose competencies are mainly firm-specific will be more limited in their adaptability outside the firm's environment, whereas an individual with generic competencies will have wider opportunities. In a contemporary business environment, many competencies essential for firm-specific success are also generic, although individuals may not be aware of this and may have a limited view of their own adaptability.

In general, human capital is defined broadly as "the stock of knowledge, skills, and abilities which can potentially increase productivity and performance at work and also life in general" and bring future returns in the form of higher salaries and better employability (Hietala 2006). The definition of the means to acquire *capital* is often limited to education and training, while a broader career view also identifies the development of competence through a careful selection of job opportunities and personal relationships.

Firm-based competency	*Career competency derivatives*	*Related career and human resource management approaches*
Culture	Know-why: Identity Values Interests	Specialization Team building Organisational career development
Know-how	Know-how: Knowledge Skills Ability	Job analysis Job design Performance appraisal Training and development
Networks	Know-whom: Inter-firm Relations Intra-firm Relations Professional and Social Relations	Interpersonal relations Customer relations Mentoring programmes

Figure 2: The relationships among firm competencies, career competencies, and common approaches in career and human resource management (Defillippi and Arthur 1994: 310)

Figure 2 reflects the dominant view of the late 1900s. It was argued that a major influence on the development of career competencies was through development activities in organisations that enabled involvement with a range of work situations and people as well as through reward policies that reinforced this development (Defillippi and Arthur 1994). Organisational culture was seen, and is still often seen, as a major influence on an employee's sense of identity, interests, and motivation - which are all important factors that make individuals *know why* they are involved. Knowledge management strategies relate to *know-how* competencies involving knowledge, skills, and expertise. *Know-whom* competencies are linked to meetings, on-site visits, and company communication and have considerable consequences for the company's reputation and its operations. There was an expectation within this that compatible individuals would be selected into the organisation and sufficiently developed in these competencies in order to meet organisational requirements.

In response to the model depicted above, Defillippi and Arthur (1994) argue that its organisational basis for the development of career competencies is a major limitation with regard to the application of the career capital concept, since it ignores the development of professional and entrepreneurial career identities, skills, and networks. There are mechanisms which assist in the development of career capital that go beyond organisations. These include occupational associations, which provide opportunities for sharing the *knowing* of *why*, *how*, and *whom* and, also, as we will show in a later section, involvement of governments wishing to increase employment of older women. The more organisations struggle to adapt to changing environments, the more their requirements of individuals and their expectations of the individual's adaptability will increase. Some individuals may become part of a core employee group with long-term organisational prospects, and others may join a peripheral, casual, on-demand, performance-contingent workforce.

This fact has important implications for individuals. Only recently, Dickman and Harris (2005) have highlighted how a variety of types of international assignments have been used by organisations to develop their employees' career capital. However, the HRM processes associated with these assignments have often been so poorly managed that individuals have not been able to recognise the correlation between their experiences and the organisational context. Vance 2005 argues that individuals do not need to rely on their organisations and can manage and initiate their own international career development.

The protean and boundaryless career concepts bring to attention the need for individuals to be aware of their values, that is, the need to *know why* they value a particular type of career involvement as much as *why* a particular task is important - for themselves or for an employer - to succeed. The individual also needs to be self-directed, that is, they need to *know how* to position themselves in order to achieve their preferred career involvement and to gain the required job competencies with a task, firm, or context-specific objective.

Lastly, it is crucial to recognise that *knowing-whom* competencies belong to the individual as well as to the organisation, and the selective use of non-hierarchical, industry-based networks can assist their careers as well as organisational purposes. Most importantly, Defillippi and Arthur (1994) conclude that the value of an individual's career competencies is "not intrinsic but is dependent on their being employed in settings that recognise their potential contribution and provide corresponding opportunities" (ibid.: 310).

In a later section of this paper, we will assess how these competencies are being promoted to assist older women in Austria and Australia who wish to continue in employment. First of all, however, we will examine the contextual factors which can influence their work options.

Employment and Career in Austria and Australia

In the preceding section we discussed the different forms of career systems identified some 20 years ago by Sonnenfeld and Peiperl (1988) as well as the concepts of boundaryless and protean careers, which try to redefine certain factors with regard to contemporary career management. Several essential issues emerged, including new styles of organisation involving a wider range of employment conditions and movement across organisations. More recently, Bright and Pryor (2005) have argued that the wide range of influences exerted on careers include unplanned and chance events that occur throughout the individual's total life-space and create a highly complex and chaotic situation. In this section, we will assess conditions both in Austria and Australia which provide examples of some such changes by focussing on two aspects, (1) workplace regulation of wages and working conditions and (2) access to age pensions, which will illustrate the fundamental differences between Austria and Australia.

The first issue we will examine is the extent to which wages and working conditions are regulated and the impact these regulations have on employment options. Information obtained from two successive OECD reports (2005a, 2005b) indicates that policies as well as certain institutions play a large role in determining employment rates of all age-groups in both countries. In general terms, there are two possible approaches when it comes to improving employment options for older women – one is enhanced regulation of employment conditions, for example, by setting wage levels, by recognising seniority, by regulating working hours, and by limiting lay-off or redundancy options. The second approach is to deregulate employment conditions, so that labour market demand and the employee's competence determine wages, hours, and stability of employment rather than seniority.

Amid much controversy, the second option has become widespread in Australia over the last ten or more years, since there has been a change from collective bargaining agreements based on occupational classifications to workplace agreements negotiated by each organisation with their workforce, and again, more recently, to individual work contracts at any level within the organisation. Negotiating individual work arrangements, of course, offers more flexibility for employers, and wage growth has been at low levels except in industries where increased demand and profitability have increased the willingness of employers to offer more. Trade union membership has declined, and the role of unions in negotiating employment agreements has become less important.

It appears that similar trends can be observed in Austria, although official collective agreements provide the legislative context of workplace negotiations. There is more regulation in that collective agreements are negotiated through the Chambers of Commerce and Labour in which membership is obligatory and the structure is legally determined, and also through voluntary representations by Trade Unions (Müller 2002; Runggaldier 2006). However, in Austria, individual company agreements (i.e. work agreements) concluded between the company owner/employer and the Works Council are increasing in number, particularly in privatised government organisations (Runggaldier 2006). Pay levels are excluded from these agreements, which is not the case in Australia.

A further difference is evident in the coverage of contracted labour conditions through labour hire companies. In Austria, this has been addressed by a collective agreement, whereas in Australia this is mostly covered by individual work contracts. Other employees, such as atypical employees and causal staff, workers with an economic but not a personal employment relationship, and self-employed staff are outside the scope of Austrian labour law and must negotiate their own employment conditions, as they do in Australia. Like in Australia, the use of such employees has increased in recent years to minimise social security and employment costs and increase employers' flexibility (Runggaldier 2006; Hauff 2007; Keller 2007). Another change similar to those in Australia is the increasing dissatisfaction with the seniority principle in determining wage levels, since the application of this principle increases the costs of older employees just because they are older, rather than because of their competence, contribution, and labour demand.

The OECD report (2005a) notes that full-time and life-time employment is becoming less secure in various industries in Austria, and that changing patterns of family life in combination with employers' demands have interacted to create significant growth in flexible or irregular types of employment. Like in Australia, much of the employment growth in the past two decades has concerned part-time employment, particularly among women. In contrast to most other countries, however, part-time work is less frequent among older workers than among prime-age workers (OECD 2005a). In Austria, regional mobility of labour is low and so small firms can provide cyclical employment without the risk of losing their labour market. However, like in Australia, there has been a significant transfer of labour-intensive and low to medium technology industries to cheaper countries. At the same time, high value-added work has expanded since the mid 1990s providing more long-term employment stability for qualified salary earners and, hence, more security for members of this section of the labour force. Consequently, employment rates are relatively high for prime-age workers of both sexes up to and including the 50-54 age-group. Yet, older workers have a higher unemployment rate because they are over-represented in declining industries, and they have a much lower level of educational attainment than members of the younger generations (OECD 2005a). For the future generation of older female workers opportunities and experiences may be somewhat different from those of the present generation.

In Australia, the unemployment rate is between 2-4 % for over 55-year-old men and women, and labour shortages are creating new opportunities for older workers across the labour market (ABS 2008). In Austria, opportunities vary more widely as the labour supply is still abundant in major occupations and skill segments, and prospects are considerably better in occupations where growth has occurred in recent years. One of the challenges, therefore, will be to prepare workers of all ages in such a way that they are able to transfer from shrinking sectors of the economy to growing ones (OECD 2005b).

Older Workers: Work and Retirement

The previous section has identified some disparate trends and similarities concerning the projected problems and issues related to older women's access to late working life in Australia and Austria. In this context, it is important to consider broader factors that might influence their desire to work. There are fundamental differences between Austria and Australia regarding the rationale for the provision of retirement income for older persons, and, consequently, the structures of the two systems are quite different. The general circumstances pertaining to retirement income in Australia are outlined in another chapter of this book (cf. Clarke, Hartmann, and Patrickson). Therefore, the comments in this chapter will focus on the system in Austria and how it compares to that in Australia.

Both in Austria and Australia, effective (that is, *actual*) and official retirement ages for women are almost the same - as opposed to many EU countries where early retirement of approximately five years is widespread. Interestingly, however, while the official retirement age for men in Austria is 65, the effective retirement age is 60 (OECD 2005a: 66). Figure 3 shows how the participation rate of Austrian men aged 60-64 has nevertheless increased from 12 % to nearly 20 % between 1995 and 2003, while the participation rate of women belonging to the same age-group has remained steady at about 5 %. However, in Australia (Figure 4) the participation rate of men in the same age-group has been steady at about 50 % for the last 20 years, and the participation rate of women aged 60-64 has risen by 10 % to 17 % since 1995.

The clear differences between the two countries regarding the participation rates of older workers can be investigated from the perspective of retirement income options and, at a later point, in terms of work options.

OECD (2005a) reports indicate that, in Austria, the purpose of the government's pension scheme has been to maintain the individual's standard of living pre and post retirement. The scheme was set up in 1956 and has, since then, been adjusted many times, but it has not been changed fundamentally. It provides an earnings-related old-age pension for workers with at least 15 insurance years, accessible from age 65 for men and from age 60 for women. It incorporates various and changing forms of early retirement as well as a derived survivor's pension for widows, widowers, orphans, and divorcees with a judicial claim to alimony. Occupational pensions are of minor relevance (and play a less important role than in most other OECD countries), as more than 90 % of all pensions are paid out of this public, first-pillar scheme.

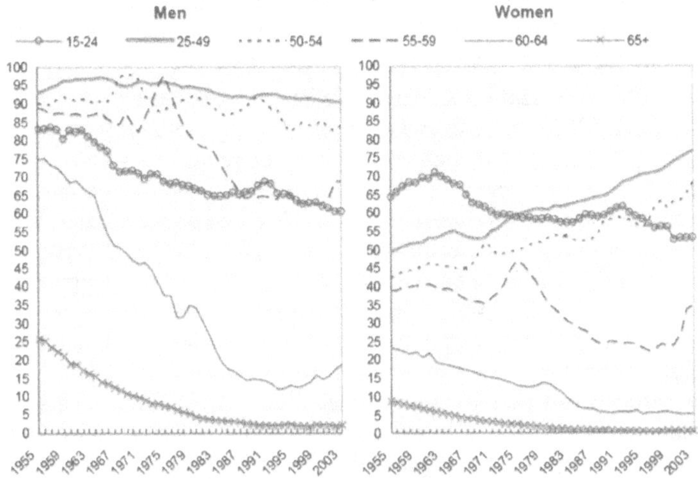

Figure 3: Participation rates in Austria by age and gender: 1955-2003 (percentages; OECD 2005a:62)

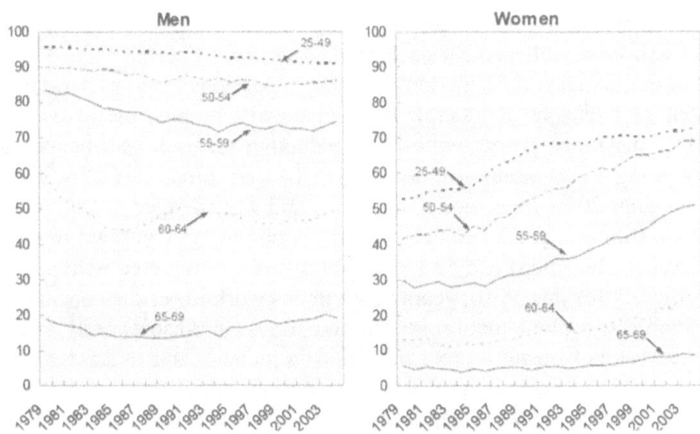

Figure 4: Participation rates in Australia by age and gender: 1979-2003 (percentages; OECD 2005b:42)

High-income earners in the private sector need to have private retirement savings because of a ceiling at about twice the average income, above which neither contributions are paid nor benefits received. Similarly, civil servants have a separate pension scheme with slightly higher income replacement rates, and the same holds true for professionals who have their own organisational pension schemes. The OECD report emphasises that new private and occupational pension schemes are unlikely to become important influences on retirement behaviour. In contrast to this, in Australia, taxation reductions for investment superannuation schemes have turned them into an attractive vehicle for accruing wealth.

In 2000, early retirement on the basis of reduced work capacity was abolished in Austria, and, by 2003, more than two-thirds of all new retirees were employed before drawing a pension, although 40 % of all men retired early on account of their long insurance record. The pension reform of 2005 established a unified pension system to include the entire labour force and is based on the rules of the previous scheme concerning private sector employees and the self-employed. The difference between the minimum early retirement age for men and women will be reduced progressively from five years to two years by 2017 (By then, women will no longer be able to retire before the age of 60.), and will be eliminated by 2033. In consistence with past practice, pensions will be equal to 80 % of the revalorised lifetime earnings to a person retiring at age 65 who has accumulated 45 insurance years, and pensions will be adjusted in line with the consumer price index. However, the latest pension reforms mean that, by 2028, the calculation of income replacement pension rates will change to one based on life-time earnings rather than on the best 15 income years. Consequently, replacement rates will generally be lower for career workers with steep increases in earnings. As women tend to have more moderate salary increases, they may benefit from this change. A pension account will be established for each insured person to permit valorised contributions and entitlements through non-contributory periods (such as periods of unemployment or intensive childcare). Retirement will be possible at the age of 62 (with 37.5 insurance years), with 4.2 % reduction for each year below age 65. A corresponding 4.2 % bonus will be given in the first three years of retirement after 65 years. Until 2010, men aged 55 and over and women aged 50 and over with 45 and 40 contribution years respectively will continue to be entitled to early retirement from age 60 (men) and 55 (women) onwards. Many men with uninterrupted careers qualify for this. Also, years of strenuous work lower the pension eligibility age. In contrast to the situation in other countries, in Austria, early exit from the workforce has not meant a great reduction in income, and retrenchment was not seen as an act of discrimination either by workers or by their institutional representatives. Only in 2004 did age discrimination become illegal.

In contrast to Austria, where pension amounts are closely related to pre-retirement income levels, the purpose of the Australian age pension payment is to provide a minimum standard of living which is paid to everyone after a certain age (and which is subject to certain income and assets tests). The amount is unrelated to previous salaries, and there are no specific contributions. In 2003, 54 % of the age eligible population received the full age pension (OECD 2005b: 67). A second tier of pension, called superannuation, which was directly linked to a person's employment status, applied to public employees. Frequently, it also concerned employees of large organisations, but, generally, not those of smaller organisations or non-managerial employees. This tier of superannuation has now largely been superseded by a third tier of investment-related superannuation. Both these types of superannuation can be accessed after age 55 rather than at the considerably later age needed for the age pension. Provided a minimum income level is reached, there is a legal requirement for a specified minimum percentage of income to be paid by employers into a superannuation fund chosen by the individual. A large number of profit-driven investment funds have been created over the last 20 years, as well as "industry-based" funds in which members elect the board, and there are no other investors. For example, Unisuper is a superannuation fund for university staff and their spouses, and similar funds have been established for people working in government, health, and education services. Each individual decides on the nature of the risk and on the type of investment for their superannuation savings. Thus, the process of funding retirement through personal savings and investment growth has become well established. In 2007, measures were taken to make age pension/superannuation income tax free for all citizens over 60 years of age, and changes to asset and income limitations made it easier to receive at least a part-age pension and the supplementary health and other benefits that go with it.

In both Australia and Austria, the increasing life expectancies of those who are entitled to receive age pensions have put pressure on the government pension funds' ability to meet these payments. Consequently, the option of gradual retirement is an idea that is being actively pursued in Australia and becoming increasingly relevant in Austria. However, in Austria, part-time work and a reduced income prior to retirement can reduce pension payments and are, therefore, financially disadvantageous. In Australia, taking retirement income and still working part-time in a gradual retirement process is viewed as an option to help people increase their financial assets for retirement and to retain older workers in the workforce. The government provides a small subsidy for superannuation contributions made by older workers with a low income.

A common feature of the public pension scheme in Austria as well as of the investment-based funds in Australia is that women and others who have gaps in employment and who do not find the means to continue to make payments to pension funds will be disadvantaged at retirement. Men with continuous careers are likely to accumulate more retirement wealth. In Australia, married couples receive less age pension than two single people, and widows are classified as single persons for government age pension assessment. In second tier organisational/salary-based superannuation systems the widow of a man who received a salary-linked benefit receives a reduced pension similar to that of an Austrian widow without her own pension. Women who have short working lives and rely on their spouses' employment-based pensions receive a reduced income if they are widowed, whereas a man's pension is not altered if his spouse dies. The increasing life expectancy of men, therefore, results in a financial advantage to married women with limited working lives. However, in most of the now dominant third tier investment-based superannuation pensions, funds are preserved as part of the owner's estate and are, therefore, most likely to be accessible to a widow or widower without any reductions.

Hence, apart from personal and emotional advantages associated with continuing to work or maintaining a career interest, there are basic financial reasons for women, who now have a life expectancy of 85 or more years, to continue to work. The career decisions that women make have significant long-term impacts on their financial status in these long retirement years. Again, some significant differences appear to be evident between Australia and Austria with regard to the extent to which women are able to take advantage of their late working lives in order to enjoy their careers and to accrue financial assets.

As mentioned earlier in this paper, in Australia, where labour shortages are evident in both the skilled and the unskilled/casual sectors of the workforce, the government campaign to encourage organisations to employ older workers is omnipresent on television and in the print media. The government's efforts to promote older people's employment is facilitated by the fact that the social security system requires all unemployed persons to actively seek work or risk loss of unemployment benefits. Recent changes permitting receipt of both a work income as well as a private pension income encourage older workers to remain working, at least part-time, prior to receiving age pension. Tax free retirement incomes from age 60 on means that self-funded retirees pay no or low taxes on any extra work income. The Australian government has, thus, tried to make it profitable for older workers to continue to work. (Such a policy has not been applied to other social security benefits.) In Austria, however, due to the generous early retirement options, many older employees and their employers have not attached much value to updating and upgrading employees' skills or maintaining their work capacities, and pensions can be reduced if they take partial retirement (OECD 2005a). Yet, the OECD (2005b) report on Australia contends that improving financial incentives for employees to remain employed longer, even if supplemented by encouraging employers to be more receptive to an age-diverse workforce, may still not be successful in creating more opportunities for older workers, unless their level of employability can be maintained and improved. Older workers who have poor health or face unsuitable work conditions will have difficulties remaining in employment. More importantly, they need empowerment through opportunities to maintain and develop their skills and access to efficient employment services and career advice. In Austria, there are a variety of government-supported labour market programmes which aim to provide just these services as well as programmes within not-for-profit and business organisations that focus on the education and the development of all groups of employees. In

Australia, government-supported initiatives are mainly directed at job seekers who are receiving government income support, including older workers who can be brought together with organisations which are experiencing difficulties in recruiting labour.

Career Capital Theory Implications for Older Working Women

Practical examples of career capital competencies can be derived by examining how they apply to older women in specific situations. For example, in Austria, with its extended hospitality industry, it is not uncommon for an older woman to manage her home as a small guest house. *Knowing why* would involve understanding the following factors: (1) why she would wish to continue to meet the demands associated with this role, (2) the impact which time and personal contacts have as she becomes older, (3) the appropriateness of financial rewards, and (4) why some tasks must be done and when. *Knowing how* might mean to understand the local labour market, the various forms of marketing, customer expectations, how to keep back-up staff available, and how to balance customers' expectations against costs. *Knowing whom* could relate to establishing networks to provide assistance with marketing and casual workers, to contributing to local government promotion committees, and, in consistence with her understanding of *knowing why*, to managing these time commitments in line with her life style preferences. Similarly, an older teacher in Australia would need to be aware of her motivation for continuing full-time or part-time permanent employment rather than casual work or retirement, of any physical, intellectual, or psychological issue arising from her age, as well as of how she will adapt to changing student characteristics and varying school/government expectations in education. *Knowing how* would involve expertise developed over her career in following or developing curricula, in maintaining students interested, in dealing with parents, difficult students, and other staff, and in managing workload peaks. *Knowing whom* could involve academic and personal support in keeping up-to-date and in interpreting and influencing policy developments. It could also involve academic networking regarding other employment opportunities and help from the community in bringing resources into class. An older woman factory worker would need to *know why* she is undertaking this work, what the implications are as she becomes older, and what her employer's as well as her own expectations are for the future. *Knowing how* would require identifying her competencies and her contribution to the organisation, not only regarding specific job demands but also her relations with other staff, producers, and customers as well as her participation in opportunities for consultation. The *knowing-whom* component may arise from her long employment in the organisation and from her place in the community, which enables her to connect with other potential employees and customers and which provides her with the knowledge about how things are done in different organisations and in sections within her organisation.

With these three examples, each employment relationship is different and covers a different time-span, but in each case the breadth of the job can be narrow or quite broad depending on the job-holder and the employer. Women who operate within a narrow perception of their job may miss opportunities for development of competencies as well as the opportunity to be able to contribute historical knowledge to their working community in their later working lives. Older women can find themselves in two types of situations: The first situation may occur when they need to maintain their credibility in their chosen, long-term domain of employment/business in response to changes in the work place or to perceptions of themselves as older women. The second situation may arise when the owner of the guest house, the teacher, or the factory worker finds that the demand for her services has declined – a new type of accommodation has become popular, the local student population has declined or their educational interests have changed, or when the factory has moved to Romania.

Changing labour market circumstances indicate that such situations are not uncommon and that employment is likely to be less stable – at least until demand in a specific segment of the labour market becomes tighter. An important option for older women may be to identify and take advantage of growing employment sectors in order to maximise their opportunities and to understand which types of career contracts employers want as well as which segments they are in or can move to. The trend toward individual contracts seems likely to continue, and women need to be able to negotiate their employment conditions. Under the given circumstances, an older woman may need to deal with a situation in which her business community or employer indicates that her career capital (or that of her colleagues who may have been "let go") is no longer valued. Developing a successful and trusting relationship with a new employer can then be difficult (Defillippi and Arthur 1994), especially as studies, such as that by Armstrong-Stassen, and Cameron (2006), show that the career satisfaction of older female professionals and managers is influenced by the efforts their organisations make to retain them and give them challenging assignments.

In both OECD reports (2005a, 2005b) much has been written about institutional and individual factors influencing employability of older workers. The focus of this paper is on the individual perspective. In this context, employability is commonly linked to possessing the required skills, to the use of training, and involvement in life-long learning; to maintaining good health and accessibility to suitable working conditions; and, lastly, to having access to good employment services and career advice (OECD 2005b). Threats to the individual career can be connected to low competitiveness (unemployment, low wages, a stagnating career, and poor development of know-how), to health problems, or to an unfavourable work environment (poor working conditions and negative organisational climate), and to the lack of access to networks and assistance. Hietala (2006b) argues that a good career is characterised by intentional investments to minimise these risks rather than reliance on luck. Being unaware of the importance of certain issues is a career risk. For example, older workers often do not recognise the importance productivity has for both employers and the government, even though employees' wages and purchasing power are to a great extent determined by productivity (Hietala 2006b). The issue of individual responsibility for maintaining work ability and employability is reiterated in the EU (2006) report on employment of older workers. Just as employers need to review work procedures to protect the health of their workforce, employees have a responsibility to maintain their fitness for work. Such concerns may require a shift in the mindset of older workers, especially since opportunities for early exit from the workforce are becoming less available. We suggest that the concept of career capital provides an accessible framework for older workers to develop a new mindset regarding career management. *Knowing why* requires the individual to understand their own and their employer's perspective regarding their employment relationship; *knowing how* requires the individual to assess what is required and to evaluate the competencies they possess in order to meet these requirements; *knowing who* requires an understanding of their colleagues within and outside their immediate employment context. The *knowing-who* factor is important if older women are to be able to work with a range of colleagues and to access the networks and institutional programmes that will assist them to make transitions.

Conclusion

If we subscribe to the view that knowledge is power, it is clear that a thorough understanding of how employment markets work and how career options can be managed should assist older women in managing their career moves successfully and in achieving more satisfaction in their late working lives. Career models are one way of organising this information. However, a specific model must always be relevant to the context in which the individual finds herself.

In this paper we have examined the context of older women's employment in Austria and in Australia. The prevailing ideologies differ considerably, and, yet, there are clear parallels between the two countries with regard to the challenges that need to be faced and the general thrust of the solutions that are implemented. Since the difficulties with regard to skill supply and dependency ratios have advanced a little further in Australia than in Austria, attempts to increase the workforce participation of older workers and to provide them with the necessary skills to manage their career situations are better developed. At the same time, the deregulation of workplace relations has not advanced as far in Austria as it has in Australia, and more protection is available to workers due to industry and organisation-based agreements. Yet, the differences in employment opportunities and the strong emphasis on small, rural enterprises in Austria also mean that the many temporary but recurrent labour opportunities for older women may not be included in government statistics. The recent OECD (2005a, 2005b) reports have highlighted the need for older workers to understand in what way they contribute to productivity, to articulate the skills they possess, and to see the opportunities the labour market holds in store for them. To perceive these tasks as opportunities to increase their career capital through *knowing why*, *knowing how*, and *knowing whom*, may be a useful framework for the empowerment of older women.

Literature

Armstrong-Stassen, M. and Cameron, S. (2006): Factors related to the career satisfaction of older managerial and professional women, in: Career Development International 10/3, 203-215.

Australian Bureau of Statistics (ABS) (2008): Labour Force, Australia, Dec 2007 – Catalogue number 6202.0. Australian Government Publishing Service, Canberra.

Baruch, Y. (2004): Transforming careers: from linear to multidirectional career paths Organizational and individual perspectives, in: Career Development International, 9. 1, 58-73.

Baruch, Y., and Peiperl, M. (2000): Career management practices: and empirical survey and implications, in: Human Resource Management, 39, 4, 347-366.

Bright, J.E.H. and Pryor, R.G. L. (2005): The Chaos Theory of Careers: A User's Guide, in: The Career Development Quarterly, 53, 291-305.

Briscoe, J.P. and Hall, D.T. (2006a): The inter-play of boundaryless and protean careers: Combinations and implications, in: Journal of Vocational Behaviour, 69, 4-18.

Clarke, M., Hartmann, L.C. and Patrickson, M. (in this book): Factors influencing work or retirement decisions for Australian women academics.

Defillippi, P. and Arthur, M. (1994): The boundaryless career: a competency based perspective, in: Journal of Organizational Behaviour 15, 307-324.

Dickman, M. and Harris, H. (2005): Developing career capital for global careers: the role of international assignments, in: Journal of World Business, 40, 399-408.

E.U. (2006): Ageing and employment: Identification of good practice to increase job opportunities and maintain older workers in employment. Final report. Director General for Employment and Social Affairs, European Union.

http://ec.europa.eu/employment_social/emplweb/news/index_en. Accessed on 31/7/07.

Hauff, S. (2007): Flexibilisierung von Beschäftigung und die Erosion psychologischer Verträge der ArbeitnehmerInnen, in: ARBEIT – Zeitschrift für Arbeitsforschung, Arbeitsgestaltung und Arbeitspolitik, 1/16, 36-53.

Hietala, K. (2006a): Human Capital. Sub-report 3, in: General framework for long term social impact evaluation of an employment strategy European commission Ministry of Labour.

Hietala, K. (2006b): Good working career. Sub-report 4, in: General framework for long term social impact evaluation of an employment strategy European commission Ministry of Labour.

Inkson, K. (2006): Protean and boundaryless careers as metaphors, in: Journal of Vocational Behaviour, 69, 48-63.

Keller, B. (ed.) (2007): Atypische Beschäftigung: Flexibilisierung und soziale Risiken, Berlin, Ed. Sigma.

Mayrhofer, W., Meyer, M. and Steyrer, H. (2005): Macht?Erfolg?Reich?Glücklich? Einflussfaktoren auf Karrieren, Wien: Linde.

Müller, M. (2002): Industrielle Beziehungen, in: Kasper, H. and Mayrhofer, W. (eds.): Personalmanagement – Führung – Organisation, Wien, Linde, 565-592.

OECD (2005a): Ageing and employment policies: Austria OECD.

OECD (2005b): Ageing and employment policies: Australia OECD.

Roehling, M.V., Cavanaugh, M.A., Moynihan, L.M. and Boswell, W.R. (2000): The nature of the new employment relationship: a content analysis of the practitioner and academic literatures, in: Human Resource Management, 39, 4, 305-320.

Runggaldier, U. (2006): The evolving structure of collective bargaining in Europe 1990-2004: National Report Austria (VS/2003/0219-SI2.359910) http://-eprints.unifi.it/arcchive/00001152/01/Austria.pdf. Accessed on 03/09/07.

Sonnenfeld, J. A. and Peiperl, M.A. (1988): Staffing policy as a strategic response: a typology of career systems, in: Academy of Management Review 13(4): 588-600.

Sullivan, S. and Arthur, M.B. (2006): The evolution of the boundaryless career concept: Examining physical and psychological mobility, in: Journal of Vocational Behaviour, 69, 19-29.

Linda Kreil

Women's Age in the Austrian Employment Law with a Special Focus on Dismissal Protection

1. Introduction

While the influence a woman's age has on employment law is perhaps not evident at first sight, a connection soon becomes apparent when paying a closer look at some of the relevant issues. In this article it will be shown that in the Austrian jurisprudence as well as in the Austrian employment law, women's age is treated differently from men's age. This can even occur, when the statute law itself does not refer to people's age at all.

Since this is the only contribution to this omnibus written from a legal perspective, certain basic law-related guidelines need to be explained first. With regard to legal matters, there are always two perspectives that need to be taken into account:

- The descriptive perspective (which may also be called the empirical or positive perspective), on the one hand, has to do with reality, i.e. with facts, which can be captured empirically. These facts can be a perspective of social reality, of individual reality, of facts in the broadest possible sense. Consequently, all the issues and questions you can prove by empirical means belong to this perspective, e.g. the difference between men's and women's incomes.
- On the other hand, there is the so-called normative perspective, which is the perspective of the law, of jurisdiction, of regulations and guidelines, e.g. the provision laid down in the EC-Treaty that there must not be a difference between the salaries men and women earn for the same or comparable work (EC-Treaty, Art 141).

Of course, these two perspectives influence each other. For example, when it was commonly believed that different wages for men and women were unfair, the legislator – in this case the EC institutions – reacted to this general conviction. The rule stating that two people have to receive the same wages for the same kind and amount of work influences the difference in income; it narrows the gap (or, at least, it is meant to narrow the gap) between men's and women's salaries. At the same time, the "real" perspective may produce an effect on the normative one, e.g. when more and more couples live together without being married (a situation which is legally referred to as cohabitation) and the legislator reacts to this in the tenancy law (which, incidentally, has not happened in Austria so far).

In my position as a lawyer I mainly interpret such provisions and regulations. I write comments on decisions of courts and tribunals. The principal assumption on my part is that a certain provision or regulation simply exists in the way it does, and the only question is how to apply it to a specific case. Therefore, in my line of work, the empirical effects of legislation or jurisdiction are not questioned in general (nor are the empirical effects which form the basis of jurisdiction). Having explained all this, I would now like to leave my own field of work and take certain legal provisions as a basis from which to take a close look at their possible effects on reality and vice versa. In particular, I will deal with dismissal and maternity protection (in Part 2 and Part 3). The article will be rounded off with some observations on the so-called "principle of seniority" (Part 4). All in all, I will try to answer the question whether women mainly receive preferential treatment or whether they are discriminated against as a result of their age in matters of legal provisions and jurisdiction in employment law. Furthermore, I will discuss possible effects this treatment has on women's role in the workplace.

2. Protection against Dismissal

a. Protection against Dismissal in General

Before dealing with its special effects on older women, a general description of the legal protection against dismissal and of how it works in Austrian law shall be given. This description is a simplified one; the mechanisms of the so-called "General Protection against Dismissal" are fairly complicated, but there are only a few principal points which need to be understood in order to fully comprehend the consequences these regulations have on older women. In addition, it has to be stressed that I merely refer to the so-called "general" protection against dismissal (§ 105 ArbVG),[1] which, however, is not the only sort of protection against dismissal in Austria. Apart from the "General Protection against Dismissal", there are special laws to protect, for instance, disabled people, pregnant women, and works council members from dismissal. Nonetheless, it is the only regulation which has an impact on older women in particular, as will be shown at a later point (in sub-chapters b and c).

The first important aspect which needs to be mentioned in this context is that, in Austria, the general principle applies that the unilateral termination of employment contracts does not need to be justified by either party: "An employer or

1 For a more detailed explanation see Guger/Runggaldier/Traxler 2000, pp150-154; for general comments on the Austrian jurisprudence concerning dismissal protection see Löschnigg 2003, pp478 -485.

employee wishing to withdraw from an employment contract that has been concluded for an unspecified duration is free to do so by giving the other party notification of his or her wish to end the legal relationship in question"[2]. Only a termination without notice needs to be justified by stating an important cause resulting from the other party's misconduct (e.g. a severe breach of confidence).

However, in an enterprise in which a works council must be established (i.e. in all organizations with five or more employees) the regulations set down by the "General Protection against Dismissal" have to be adhered to. Dismissal protection is included in the so-called Labour Constitution Act (§§ 105-107 ArbVG), which, interestingly, is not part of the Austrian constitution. It applies to the termination of an employment contract with a period of notice as well as to that without such a period, which, in fact, would be a dismissal in the narrow sense of the word. Therefore, when I use the term "dismissal", I refer to both forms of termination of the work contract. The protection against dismissal creates a claim to keep a position under certain circumstances. If an employee enforces this claim by legal action the procedure will consist of three – in particular cases of four – steps.

As a first step the employee has to prove the negative social impacts of the termination. This is the key to protection against dismissal. What is meant by this is that the dismissal must not harm the employee's interests in a substantial way. "This is especially the case when the dismissed employee is faced with the prospect of prolonged unemployment or that of considerably lower-paid work".[3] As one can see, the presumptive chances the employee has on the job market are a very important factor. In addition to that, personal factors are taken into account, e.g. whether the employee has to provide financial support for children, a spouse, or aged parents, or whether the person has other important financial charges. For example, it is regarded as socially unacceptable to dismiss a 49-year-old father of four who has just taken out a huge mortgage for buying a house (you may have noticed the gender aspect inherent in this example).

As a second step the employer can provide an economic justification of his or her decision, e.g. by stating that it was necessary because of a company re-organisation, a reduction of the production capacity, or another economic reason. In addition to such justifications, the employer may refer to personal motives, e.g. reasons connected to the employee's personal features and his or her behaviour. As a third step a tribunal has to balance the interests of each party and to decide whether the dismissal is legally valid or not. However, there can, at times, be one further measure, i.e. a fourth step: The employee may claim that the dismissal of another employee would have a less negative social impact on that employee than it would have on him- or herself, e.g., if the other employee would have better chances on the job market. Then the tribunal has to compare the social criteria

2 Guger/Runggaldier/Traxler 2000, p150.

3 Guger/Runggaldier/Traxler 2000, p151.

applying to both employees in question. Still, this procedure is only possible, if the workers' council has voiced an objection to the dismissal in a particularly regulated way.

b. Women and Age with Regard to Dismissal Protection

With regard to the employee's age, an interesting differentiation can be detected in Austrian jurisdiction: The dismissal of women is generally judged as illegal from the age of 44 on, whereas the dismissal of men is not allowed by the Austrian jurisdiction from the age of 47 on.[4] Thus, women seem to have an obvious advantage regarding their age. Of course, there are individual exceptions: A highly qualified woman of 53 may be considered to have good chances on the job market because of her qualifications, experience, and so on, whereas a man of 49 who has none of these advantages will be regarded more worthy of protection. Since these facts are taken into account, the given age criteria are more of a guideline than an exact regulation. Nonetheless, the fact that there is always room for considering individual cases should not deflect from the general observation that the Austrian dismissal protection appears to give women preferential treatment.

Now the question is: What are the reasons for this seemingly preferential treatment? One possible answer becomes apparent when having a look at the different pension ages of men and women in the Austrian pension insurance system.[5] Therefore, I will briefly outline some general points regarding the Austrian pension system: The statutory retirement age originally stood at 60 years for women and at 65 years for men. In specific cases, early retirement was possible at the age of 55 for women and at the age of 60 for men.[6] All these regulations, however, were repealed by the legislator a few years ago. In the year 2004, it was decided to assimilate men's and women's retirement ages in several steps. Nevertheless, full assimilation will not be reached until 2033.[7] The current age gap was judged to be in conformity with the EC regulations on anti-discrimination by the European Court of Justice (ECJ)[8]. Consequently, it is true that women are allowed to retire at an earlier age than men.

This, however, might be one of the reasons why women are considered 'old' or 'aged' at an earlier age than men and, as a consequence, why their reduced

4 For references of the jurisdiction cf Löschnigg 2003, p479.

5 Cf Rebhahn in Rebhahn 2005, § 3 comment no 167, who points out that, although in another context, the ECJ takes the fact that the risk of unemployment is particularly high in the years before retirement. This shows that this explanation seems to be generally accepted.

6 Guger/Runggaldier/Traxler 2000, pp200-201.

7 A critical voice in Austrian legal literature: Winkler 2002, p224.

8 European Court of Justice 23rd of May, 2000, C 1-04/98 (Buchner et al. vs Sozialversicherungsanstalt der Bauern).

chances on the labour market seem to start earlier than those of men. We need to remember that an employee's chance to benefit from dismissal protection depends on his or her potential chances to find a new job. The likelihood of finding new and adequate employment is regarded as an assessable fact which can be stated in a legal procedure, such as a tribunal, and which is provable by presenting the opinion of a labour market expert. The expert's assessment is regarded as a fact which is not subject to the judge's discretion, which means that the judge has to accept it as it is.

Thus, one can observe that the normative perspective (i.e. the regulation regarding different pension ages for men and women) has a bearing on the real perspective (i.e. the chances on the labour market), which, yet again, influences the normative perspective (i.e. the consequences on dismissal protection). In other words, a preferable form of protection against dismissal in the case of older women would be a jurisdictional reaction to their reduced chances on the labour market (no matter what the reasons for these reduced chances are).

Obviously, protection is not the problem but the facts that lie behind it. The difference in the degree of protection is justified by the facts and, therefore, is not to be criticized as unfair to men (and, in fact, you will hardly find any criticism of it in literature[9]). Rather it is to be judged as conforming to the principles of equal opportunities – such as laid down in the EC-Treaty and in the Austrian constitution.

c. The Disadvantages of Married Women Claiming Dismissal Protection

One cannot discuss women's dismissal protection without mentioning an obvious discriminatory aspect of this regulation's enforcement by the courts: If a woman is married the Austrian jurisdiction takes the spouse's income into account when judging the negative social impacts of a dismissal.[10] The basis of this can be found in the concept of spousal support (i.e. the claim of being supported by your spouse during the marriage and – in special circumstances – even after getting divorced) laid down in the Austrian family law.[11] As a consequence, this regulation is only relevant to married women. If a woman lives in cohabitation, only her own income is taken into account.

---

9 An explicitly positive view (this age difference is not discriminating against men because of their sex) is taken by Rebhahn in Rebhahn 2005, § 3 comment 162. On the other hand, a critical opinion (with regard to a similar legal provision particularly for small enterprises/branches) is supported by Mayr, RdW 2001, p26: In this opinion, the preferential treatment of women might be discriminating against men.

10 E.g. OGH 19th of December 2001, RdW 2002, p358; OGH 16th of December 2005, ASoK 2006, p368; OLG Wien 17th of August 2005, ARD no 5671/4/2006.

11 § 94 ABGB (General Civil Code); §§ 66 – 80 EheG (Marriage Act).

In legal terms, this seems to be fair – at least at first sight. Jurisdiction takes into account every family-related legal duty which has effects on the employee's income as well as every financial burden the person has to bear, e.g. maintenance claims between parents and – even grown up – children. The law only considers whether a legal duty exists or not, and, if there is one, whether you can put it enforceable at law or not (e.g. when the debtor is insolvent). Hence, if you are married to someone who earns a good income, your dismissal protection decreases or even ceases to exist – no matter whether you are a woman or a man.

Usually, however, this jurisdiction brings about a clear disadvantage for women, because of the general gap between men's and women's incomes. Therefore, the risk of losing your job due to the sufficiently high income your spouse earns will, in general, be much higher if you are a married woman than if you are a married man – no matter how old you are. Of course, this is no matter of age, but one that applies to all married women. However, if we take into account the fact that the protection against dismissal is – among other things – a question of age, one can say that a 50-year-old married woman has a higher risk of losing her job than a 50-year-old married man.

The whole issue seems to be a matter of indirect discrimination against women. However, ignoring the critical comments on the discrimination inherent in women's dismissal protection in academic literature,[12] the Austrian Supreme Court of Justice (OGH) and, correspondingly, the Austrian Labour Courts, did not change their jurisdiction with regard to this inconsistency. At this point, a digression to social security has to be made: Interestingly, the same inconsistency occurs in connection with the Austrian unemployment support (Notstandshilfe).[13] Like dismissal protection, this social security benefit may be refused as a result of the spouse's income (and, in this case, even as a result of the partner's income in the case of cohabitation). The Austrian Administrative Court (VwGH) ruled that this is consistent with the EC anti-discrimination regulation.[14]

12 E.g. Eichinger, RdW 2002, p347; Gahleitner in Cerny/Gahleitner/Preiss/Schneller 2005, § 105 comment no 36 (p372); Rebhahn in Rebhahn 2005, § 3 comment no 164. Contrary opinion: Grillberger in Bydlinski/Mayer-Maly 2005, p38.

13 The unemployment support differs from the unemployment benefit (Arbeitslosengeld). The unemployment benefit is given to the unemployed person in the first 20 weeks of his/her unemployment, and it does not matter if he or she has other financial sources. If the unemployed person does not find any job after that time, he or she will obtain just the unemployment support (Notstandshilfe), which is clearly lower and bound to some conditions.

14 VwGH 14th of January 2004, reference no 2002/08/0202 (unpublished); VwGH 18th of February, 2004 ARD no 5526/17/2004; VwGH 17th of March 2004, ARD no 5526/18/2004; for details of the Austrian regulation and its enforcement cf VwGH 24th of January 2006 infas 2007/no S 30 (p119); VwGH 20th of September 2006, RdW 2007/no 588 and others. For (critical) comments on this cf Mayr, DRdA 2003, p199; Mayr, RdW 2002, p672 (The latter includes a remark on the negative impacts on the pension claims of women but, meanwhile,

Of course, the example described above deals with a slightly different situation because, as opposed to dismissal protection, the unemployment support is – at least at first glance – a social security benefit, and one may ask if somebody who has a legal claim on financial support by his family members should get this benefit from the public. Still, we are left with serious doubts: The Austrian unemployment support is a matter of social insurance and not of social welfare (Sozialhilfe). This means that women who benefit from this insurance contributed to it in the past.[15]

In my opinion, we are dealing with an unjustified and most unsatisfactory situation here because regulations like the ones mentioned above are at odds with women's financial security on base of their own incomes, their independence from their spouses, and their professional opportunities. To change this situation would be a clear signal on part of the Austrian legislator – or on part of the European Court of Justice – and, therefore, more than necessary. However, I very much doubt whether the Austrian legislator will reconsider its position because, by and large, there seems to be very little awareness regarding these inconsistencies.

If the jurisdiction was to be changed in the way proposed here, this could, at first sight, have rather peculiar effects in some cases: A woman who is financially secure would keep her job and her family would keep its double income, while another person (man or woman) may lose his or her job although he or she is the sole bread-winner of the family because this person has some other reasons why he or she is taken out of dismissal protection (e.g. more property).

First of all, we have to ask ourselves why someone in possession of more property should not get less protection than someone with less property. It is always a matter of the specific case whether a dismissal has highly negative social impacts or not. One should consider, too, that an employee's severance pay (Abfertigung) is not taken into account either. The severance pay is a special payment which the employer has to make to the employee in the event of a termination of the employment relationship. In its old version this payment can even amount to a year's salary. The same holds for the Austrian unemployment benefit (Arbeitslosengeld), which, again, is not regarded as relevant because it is a kind of social benefit. As one can see, there are examples of financial support which are not taken into account when judging the negative social impacts of a dismissal.

---

this odd consequence has been abolished by the legislator, cf § 34 AlVG in the current version). For more examples cf Krapf, DRdA 2007, p412; and for more detailed information Pülzl, ASoK 2005, p154. – There are similar provisions in Germany, which even take the income of a partner into account if the partners are not married, but live in cohabitation. For the German jurisdiction cf Bundesverfassungsgericht (Federal Constitutional Court) 28th of September 2005, NZS 2006, p201; Landessozialgericht (Regional Social Court) Sachsen-Anhalt, 22nd of April 2005, NZS 2006, p262.

15 There is a particular quota for women, but it refers to age and other criteria (cf Krapf/Keul, ARD 2006). Therefore, the problem does not cease to exist.

At the end of this chapter dealing with the treatment of older women in the context of the Austrian "General Protection against Dismissal", I would like to summarize the two major observations that have been made: Firstly, women in general fall under this protection at a younger age than men and, therefore, receive preferential treatment. Secondly, married women receive less protection because their spouse's incomes are taken into account. The former seems to be a matter of fact and is accepted by scientific literature as non-discriminating against men, whereas the latter possesses discriminating elements and has, for that reason, been criticized by several experts.[16]

3. Maternity Protection

The impact a woman's age has on legal regulations can also be observed in the context of maternity protection, which forms part of the Austrian employment law. After all, the general topic of this volume, women and age, does not only include women of old age, but also younger women and some of their specific problems.

In the case of maternity protection, it is not the law itself that makes a difference between age groups, but the employer's reaction to it: Young women can become pregnant and this can be their great disadvantage in the eyes of the employer. This, in turn, is a common argument which certainly has a considerable influence on recruitment policies. The fact that a woman's (young) age negatively influences her chances of employment is, of course, illegal according to EC anti-discrimination provisions, but – as we all know – it is part of every-day working life. More central to my argumentation, however, is the fact that this practice is probably unjustifiable even by business standards and if you apply very hard financial criteria.

To demonstrate this, I would like to compare some important legal regulations which are part of maternity protection on the one hand and the legal regulations dealing with the termination of an employment relationship on the other.

To begin with, I will give a short overview of the regulations concerning maternity protection in Austria:[17] An expectant mother has to inform her employer of her pregnancy without delay as soon as she knows about it herself. In addition to that, "there is an absolute ban on the employment of expectant mothers during a period of eight weeks prior to their expected date of confinement and during a period of

16 This seems to be contradictory: Why should the first be a matter of fact and the second one not? This might be an interesting question, but the preferential treatment of women has nothing to do with their discrimination. One can, as a matter of fact, ask if it as a form of discrimination against men. However, this cannot be part of the present article.

17 §§ 3-9 MSchG (Maternity Protection Act); for more detailed information cf Burger-Ehrnhofer/ Schrittwieser/Thomasberger 2007.

eight weeks (or in certain cases up to 16 weeks) following the actual date of confinement"[18].

Before this period of absolute protection "they may not be assigned to types of work that are harmful to their own physical well-being or to that of their unborn child". Night-work, work on Sundays and public holidays, working overtime, as well as every other work which includes "a risk to the life and health of the expectant mother or her unborn child" – all this is illegal. In addition to that, the young mother is entitled to take the time for breast-feeding her child during paid working hours (in two 45-minute nursing-sessions in the course of an eight-hour working day) – a practically negligible provision. Apart from these special regulations, the expectant as well as the young mother has to accomplish her contractual duties as an employee as efficiently as all her colleagues.

Due to the strict regulations regarding the announcement of a pregnancy, the employer has several months to react to the new situation, for instance by finding a substitute for the weeks before and after confinement. Furthermore, in the period of absolute protection, the employer does not have to pay a salary to the woman; she receives "maternity benefit" (Wochengeld), a special health insurance benefit. After this period of compulsory non-employment has expired, mothers (or, subject to certain conditions, fathers) are entitled to take unpaid (!) parental leave until the child reaches the age of two.[19] In larger organizations they are entitled to opt for working part-time. Within the complete period of maternity protection special protection against dismissal applies to them.

At this stage, we have to look at the possibilities to terminate an employment relationship in general. As I mentioned before, a contract of unlimited duration can be terminated at any given time by giving the other party notification. "The sole requirement is that in doing so [one] must observe the period between notice and termination date specified by the law, by a collective agreement, or, possibly, in an individual contract. (The period of notice is the minimum period of time that must elapse between the receipt of notification of termination by the other party and the end of the employment relationship.) In the case of white-collar workers, the statutory period of notice to be observed by the employee is only one month, and the termination date (which is the earliest possible date at which such notice of termination may start to take effect) is the end of the one-month-period. In the case of blue-collar workers, the period of notice is even shorter: There is a negotiable notification period of 14 days provided for, which is usually shortened or lengthened by collective agreement."[20] In the case of a contract of limited duration, there are no such notification periods at all. The contract automatically ends on the last day of the provided duration if one of the parties refuses to elongate it.

18 Guger/Runggaldier/Traxler 2000, p32.

19 Guger/Runggaldier/Traxler 2000, pp32-33.

20 Guger/Runggaldier/Traxler 2000, pp150-151.

When one compares these notification periods one can see that there is much more time left for looking for a substitute in the case of a maternity protection period than in the case of an employee's notice of termination. An employee can, after all, leave an organization for whatever reasons he or she has and only has to adhere to a rather short period of notice. Besides, the employer's expenses in the case of maternity protection are lower than those of regular sick-leave, because, as mentioned above, the main costs are borne by the social security system.

To me there seems to be a common misconception regarding the disadvantages an employee's pregnancy causes for the employer.[21] The only concrete disadvantage is the special protection against dismissal applicable to expectant mothers (or young parents during their parental leave or their part-time work). This, I have to admit, may considerably restrict the employer's flexibility in recruiting and decruiting. Apart from that, however, one always has to bear in mind that every employee can leave a company easily within a few weeks only, whereas there are approximately three months at least in which the employer can find someone to occupy the vacant position of an expectant mother.

What I am trying to explain is that, while there is a thing called maternity protection in the Austrian employment law which may create slight risks for the employer, there is still no reason to regard this regulation as a catastrophe, as seems to be done by most employers. In addition to termination by notice, sick-leave, or other absences, it is just one of the challenges an employer has to face.

4. The Principle of Seniority

One final issue which needs to be addressed here is the so-called principle of seniority in connection with pay categories and the differences it may cause between men's and women's salaries when employees become older.

In Austria this principle represents "an important criterion with respect to pay increases both in the public service and in the private sector. In the private sector, the principle is established for white-collar workers in manufacturing industry by collective agreement. In this case, each pay grade (defined on the basis of job demands and skill requirements) is subdivided into several bands of so called years of service in grade, representing the individual employee's length of service with the employer concerned in that grade. The longer an individual has worked

21 A good, or better to say, a bad example can be found in an article by Christian Scholz in the Austrian newspaper Der Standard 2007, pK43. The author raises the question whether it is justifiable from a competitive view-point that certain organisations face financial disadvantages just because they employ women, who might become pregnant (author's own translation). He does not reflect on the facts behind this common "knowledge", but obviously takes them for granted.

for the same employer, the higher they rise within the pay grade, with an automatic increase every two years."[22] In the last ten years, the seniority principle has become less important notably because of the tendency to increase minimum starting salaries and to decrease the effect the length of service has on progressive pay rises. Nonetheless, this principle is still very common in Austrian practise.

In the year 2000, an EC Council Directive[23] defined the principle of equal treatment; it means that there shall be no direct or indirect discrimination based on religion or belief, disability, age, or sexual orientation with regard to employment and occupation. Apart from that, of course, the prior principle of the equal treatment of men and women is still valid. Mainly in the year 2003, a discussion focusing on a possible contradiction between this principle on the one hand and that of seniority on the other arose in academic literature as well as in politics.

The question is whether the principle of seniority is, in fact, a form of discrimination on the basis of age in which younger employees are being discriminated against. After all, discrimination based on age does not only refer to the discrimination of older people but also to cases of unfair treatment of younger people because of their age.[24] The predominant opinion seems to be that age discrimination does not pose a problem if the salary level is connected to so-called objective criteria, like professional experience or length of service with an organization, and not to an employee's biological age.[25] I have to admit that I supported this opinion in a publication dealing with this problem.[26] While doing so, however, I did not consider that this might cause disadvantages for older women. It is easy to understand that many of them will meet fewer of these objective criteria than men because of the predictable interruptions in their careers.[27] Should the seniority principle, therefore, mainly focus on professional experience rather than on age? Or does this mean a specific discrimination against older women? It is not easy to give a clear answer to these questions. As a consequence, I would like to merely add some of my observations to the current discussion.

First of all, focusing on professional criteria only would be highly unfair if they were considered a means to keep women from receiving benefits. This might be the case if, for instance, the wages in a given organization were raised considerably in connection with the length of service in unqualified jobs, which do not

22 Guger/Runggaldier/Traxler 2000, p190.

23 Council Directive no 2000/78/EC of November 27th, 2000, establishing a general framework for equal treatment in employment and occupation.

24 Windisch-Graetz in Rebhahn 2005, § 17.

25 Windisch-Graetz in Rebhahn 2005, § 20 comment no 32 with reference to the ECJ.

26 Runggaldier/Kreil, RdW 2003, p394.

27 The ECJ ruled that the time of maternity protection has to be counted as a period of active service (cf Rebhahn in Rebhahn 2005, § 3 comment no 140). This, however, is only applicable to maternity leave, and not to any other typical interruption in a woman's career.

have any need of professional experience and if women in that particular plant have a perceptible disadvantage from that. Such a case would clearly fall into the EC anti-discrimination jurisdiction.[28]

However, if professional experience is an actual criterion in a particular case, it must not be estimated as unfair. In such cases, the problem has to be searched for elsewhere: women in general have to get the same chances as men to obtain the same amount of professional experience and/or length of service within a company. If this is obviously not the case, this, in my opinion, is a signal that the social system itself does not function properly: here the issue of the encouragement and support of women's careers arises, in particular questions concerning adequate child care options, women's education and training, and so on. This, however, is, as I have mentioned before, a matter of the social system at large and, therefore, does not fall under the "normative perspective" described in the introductory passages of this article, but rather under the "descriptive perspective", which, as a consequence, will have to be changed. This can mean that both the social circumstances and the law need to be adjusted.

5. Summary

In conclusion, the three main observations concerning women's age in the context of the Austrian employment law which I have made in this paper will be recapitulated:

1. With regard to dismissal protection the decreasing chances older women have on the labour market positively influence the degree of their protection. On the other hand, however, if a woman is married, the income of her spouse influences her protection against dismissal negatively.
2. The regulations comprising maternal protection in Austria seem to cause a skewed perception and a depreciation of younger women in the minds of presumptive employers.
3. Regarding the principle of seniority so-called objective criteria, like professional experience and the length of service with a company, seem to be unfair to older women, although it is doubtful whether they would be used discriminatingly against them.

28 Rebhahn in Rebhahn 2005, § 3 comment no 141, § 20 comment no 32.

Literature

Burger-Ehrnhofer, K./Schrittwieser, B./Thomasberger, M. (eds., 2007): Kommentar zum Mutterschutzgesetz und Väter-Karenzgesetz, Wien.

Cerny, J./Gahleitner, S./Preiss, J./Schneller, H. (eds.; 2005): Kommentar zum Arbeitsverfassungsgesetz, 3rd ed., Wien.

Eichinger, J. (2002): Berücksichtigung des Ehegatteneinkommens beim Kündigungsschutz: Mittelbare Frauendiskriminierung? Recht der Wirtschaft (RdW), pp347-349.

Gahleitner, S. (2005): § 105 ArbVG, in: Cerny, J/Gahleitner, S/Preiss, S/ Schneller, H. (eds.): Kommentar zum Arbeitsverfassungsgesetz, 3rd ed., Wien, pp305-428.

Grillberger, K. (1995): Hauptprobleme des Individualarbeitsrechts, in: Bydlinski, F./Mayer-Maly, Th., Die Arbeit: Ihre Ordnung – ihre Zukunft – ihr Sinn, Wien, pp35-39.

Guger, A./Runggaldier, U./Traxler, F. (2000): European Employment & Industrial Relations Glossary: Austria, London: Sweet & Maxwell, vol. (?) of the series edited by M. Terry and T. Treu.

Krapf, G. (2007): Notstandshilfe: Anrechnung von fiktivem Partnerunterhalt, Das Recht der Arbeit (DRdA), pp412-413.

Krapf, G./Keul, J. (2006): Anrechnung des Partnereinkommens bei der Notstandshilfe, ARD no 5709/5/2006, pp5-7 (extract of Krapf, G./Keul, J., Kommentar zum Arbeitslosenversicherungsgesetz, 2nd ed.).

Löschnigg, G. (2003): Arbeitsrecht, 10th ed., Wien.

Mayr, K. (2001): Diskriminierung aufgrund des Geschlechts und Kündigung in Kleinbetrieben, Recht der Wirtschaft (RdW), pp26-28.

Mayr, K. (2002): Notstandshilfe und Partnereinkommen: Europarechtliche Gesichtspunkte, Recht der Wirtschaft (RdW), pp672-674.

Mayr, K. (2003): Anrechnung des Partnereinkommens auf die Notstandshilfe EU-widrig!?! Das Recht der Arbeit (DRdA), pp199-200.

Pülzl, P. (2005): Notstandshilfe: Leistungen aus der Arbeitslosenversicherung als anrechenbares Partnereinkommen, Arbeits- und Sozialrechtskartei (ASoK), pp154.

Rebhahn, R. (ed., 2005): Kommentar zum Gleichbehandlungsgesetz, Wien.

Rebhahn, R. (2005): § 3, in: Rebhahn, R. (ed.), Kommentar zum Gleichbehandlungsgesetz, pp90-228.

Runggaldier, U./Kreil, L. (2003): Richtlinienwidrigkeit des Senioritätsprinzips? Recht der Wirtschaft (RdW), pp394-396.

Scholz, Ch. (2007): Was die Arbeitswelt von morgen bestimmt – Anmerkungen zur Flexicurity, Der Standard: 5th/6th of May, pK43.

Windisch-Graetz, M. (2005), § 17, in: Rebhahn, R. (ed.), Kommentar zum Gleichbehandlungsgesetz, pp424-449.

Windisch-Graetz, M. (2005), § 20, in: Rebhahn, R. (ed.), Kommentar zum Gleichbehandlungsgesetz, pp464-486.

Winkler, J. (2002): Ungleiches Pensionsalter von Männern und Frauen – EU-konform? Recht der Wirtschaft (RdW), pp224-225.

Florentine Maier

Doing Hair – Doing Age: Perspectives of Emancipated Ageing

This chapter investigates how, with what consequences, and under what conditions women enact an emancipatory discourse of old age by subverting the two conventional notions of old age as a process of decline or of "successful ageing". These questions are explored within a multimodal discourse analysis of unconventional hairstyles produced for and interactions carried out with women at an Austrian avant-garde hair stylist's. The emancipatory counter-discourse of ageing, referred to as "emancipated ageing" in this chapter, is characterized by an emphasis on personality and individuality and by a resistance to conform to conventional norms of femininity, age, and sexual orientation. In contrast to prevalent discourses of old age, it enables lifelong maintenance or growth. However, evidence from the case study suggests that its prevalence is limited to a privileged social milieu, namely that of the educated urban middle class.

1 Introduction

In recent years, images of attractive, active older people – often called flattering names, like senior citizens, golden agers, or best agers – have become widespread in popular culture. Such images are replacing notions of old age as a time of decay and passivity. This change has been largely welcomed by scientists and indeed by anyone concerned with older people's wellbeing. Some authors, however, are more critical of the possibilities that contemporary discourses of "successful ageing" offer (for example Tulle-Winton 1999; McHugh 2000; Biggs 2001; Cruikshank 2003; Casalanti 2005; Laliberte Rudman 2006). In a discourse of "successful ageing", ageing is dissociated from decline (Trethewey 2001). Activity is presented as the key to health and happiness in later life (Sinding and Gray 2005; Laliberte Rudman 2006), the possibility of expanding mid-life, if not youth, and postponing old age is emphasized, and ageing is presented as a process that individuals can and should manage responsibly (Leibing 2005; Potts et al. 2006). While the discourse of "successful ageing" has opened up a new form of freedom for later life, it has also established new obligations. The individual is considered as able and, therefore, obliged to prevent decline and ensure health and activity throughout life. New standards by which older people judge themselves and are judged by others are established (Laliberte Rudman 2006).

These contrasting aspects inherent in the discourse of "successful ageing" are especially poignant in the field of beauty and the beauty industry. Modern science has multiplied the possibilities of styling the body. A wide range of practices and commercial products are now available that promise to disguise, postpone, or even reverse the bodily changes occurring with ageing (see, for example, Coupland 2007). I agree with Debbie Laliberte Rudman's (2006) contention in that the standards suggested by the discourse of "successful ageing" create unrealistic expectations on part of the people who try to work towards them. With regard to conventional feminine beauty, reaching a state of eternal mid-life, if not eternal youth, is an objective that is ultimately doomed to fail.

While it is certainly encouraging that old age is no longer equated with decay, and while the criticism of the "successful ageing" discourse is enlightening, new research focusing on old age has only begun to touch the pressing question whether there are ways of getting old comfortably and still avoid the pitfalls of the "successful ageing" concept. Recently, scholars of ageing have started to examine popular concepts of old age that subvert both the notion of age as decline as well as that of "successful ageing". For example, Annie Potts et al. (2006) have studied men's counter-stories on erectile dysfunction, and Justine Coupland and Angie Williams (2002) have explored feminist emancipatory texts on the menopause. Mei-Chen Lin et al. (2004) have examined representations of age identities in online discourse and have identified new positive sides of ageing, such as a mind-over-body attitude, wisdom, maturity, and the feeling that old age frees from socially prescribed duties and roles. In her book "Learning to Be Old" (2003), which can be placed somewhere between a practical guide to aging and a theoretical work, Margaret Cruikshank has coined the term "comfortable aging" to describe an understanding of ageing that goes beyond concepts like decline or success:

> "Comfortable aging" is preferable to successful aging because it emphasizes ease rather than external measurement, and because we can judge for ourselves whether or not we are aging comfortably. While successful aging implies that failure is possible, comfortable aging has a more neutral and nonjudgemental opposite. Comfortable aging also carries a faint hint of emancipatory hedonism, for which we have little time in youth and middle age and too little permission at any age. I would broaden the definition of "hedonism" to include the pleasures of breathing deeply and being still. (Cruikshank 2003: 3)

Books and studies like these suggest that an alternative understanding of old age is emerging. Since the meanings, metaphors, representations, images, stories, statements, etc. present in this alternative understanding of old age work together to produce a particular version of old age, they can be understood as a discourse. By discourse I mean "practices which form the objects of which they speak" (Foucault 1972: 49). A discourse of old age paints a particular picture of it; it constructs old age in a certain way. Evidence of the existence of a particular discourse can come from multiple modes of communication: from written or oral language, but also from less obvious sources, such as everyday objects, architecture, dress, or – as in this study – hairstyles (van Leeuwen 2005: 95). The newly emerging discourse of ageing, which I suggest calling "emancipated ageing", opposes dominant discourses of decay and "successful ageing" in order to produce a different version of old age potentially available through language and practices.

2 Theoretical Background and Research Question

The examination of age in this paper starts out from social constructionist foundations. Constructionist gerontology (seminal works including N. Coupland, J. Coupland and Giles 1989 and Gubrium, Holstein and Buckholt 1994) has strong parallels with constructionist gender studies (e.g. Harold Garfinkel's study on the transsexual Agnes, 1967; West and Zimmerman 1987; Butler 1990). Constructionist gerontology assumes that there is no "essence of age" that underlies the observation of age phenomena, but only the plausibility offered by the distinction between age and other things. "We don't age because our heads or brains want to, but because we explain changes in our thinking and physical processes with the category 'age'. One way to understand such changes is to decipher them as signs of ageing." (Saake 1998: 11, author's own translation)[1] The first premise of constructionist gerontology, therefore, is that age does not have an objective existence in itself.

From this follows a second premise of constructionist gerontology: Age is "made" or "done" by people in their daily interactions with real or imagined others. It is not done alone, but within social constraints. The terms that make up a person's age are outside herself, in a society that has no single author (cf. Butler 2004 on gender). However, the relationship between discourses and individual agency is circular: How people "do" their age and gender is neither dictated by discourse, nor is it totally self-determined. On the one hand, discourses define social reality and delimit what is imaginable. Even if people are aware of dominant discourses and question them personally, they may still conform to prevalent norms because they want to be acknowledged and understood by others. On the other hand, even the most dominant discourses are never without inner inconsistencies, less elaborate aspects, or contradictions with other relevant discourses. Resistance and

1 Fascinating examples of differing interpretations of physical changes are given in Andrea Sankar's (1984) comparative study of the treatment of old age in American and Chinese medicine and in Martha Holstein's (1997) history of Alzheimer's Disease and senile dementia.

change, though difficult, are therefore possible. It is only by doing age and gender that the discourses on which age and gender are based are produced and reproduced.

This leads to a third premise of constructionist gerontology: Age has tangible consequences on people's lives. The fact that age is socially constructed does not mean that it is "not real" or that "you just have to think young to be young". The consequences of constructions of old age are an important research topic of constructionist gerontology.

Against the theoretical background presented above, the research questions of this paper can be formulated as follows:

- In what way do women enact an emancipatory discourse of old age? What are the characteristics of this discourse?
- What are the effects which enacting an emancipatory discourse of old age has on older women's lives, especially in comparison to those of discourses of decay or "successful ageing"?
- What are the conditions in which an emancipatory discourse of old age can be enacted?

3 Method

As these questions are very broad, I will explore them on the basis of a specific example: that of older women who wear a certain type of very unusual hairstyle (see, for example, photographs 1 to 3). The women's hairstyles shown in these pictures were chosen because they represent a nonconformist way of ageing and can, therefore, be seen as a form of "declining to decline" (Morganroth Gullette 1997), but also because they resist conventional notions of feminine beauty as endorsed in the concept of "successful ageing". This type of hairstyle is called "Musterschnitt" in German. There is no proper English name for it; it could be called graphic cut or visual clippering. For the purpose of this paper, I will refer to this haircut as "graphic cut" because this term renders the meaning and style of the German word most accurately. A graphic cut is defined by the following characteristics: (1) The hair produces a graphic pattern or image on the head. (2) The pattern or image is located on a permanently visible place on the head – and is not, for example, covered by long hair and only visible if part of or all the hair is pinned up. (3) It is a real "cut", as the graphic patterns or images are achieved by relatively long-term modifications of the hair, such as cutting, shaving, or dying – not by removable styling products, such as gel, wax, or hairspray.

Photograph 1: Graphic cut 1

Photograph 2: Graphic cut 2

Photograph 3: Graphic cut 3

Hairstyles are an especially interesting mode of communication. There are striking similarities, but also differences, between hairstyles and verbal practices, such as talking or writing. Like talk, hairstyles are deliberately created by people. They tell something about the culture in which they are made and worn and also about the individuals who wear them. Like talk, we use hairstyles as a means of defining ourselves. They also always provide information on who we are. We and others interpret them, and these interpretations do not necessarily correspond.

In contrast to language, a hairstyle is always and necessarily a manifestation of some sort. We can adjust our talk to a given situation, but our hairstyle stays the same for a longer period of time. We might get a special hairstyle for certain occasions (e.g. for a wedding or an important job interview), but usually we wear our hairstyle for a much longer time than, for example, a particular item of clothing or make-up. Few people change their hairstyles everyday. However, hair can be manipulated fairly easily and offers a great variety of creative options (as opposed to, for example, the shape of the body). Finally, a person's hairstyle is located in a prominent place (unlike, for example, a tattoo on the arm), which makes it play an important role in almost every kind of personal interaction (cf. Janecke 2004).

The data for this analysis was gathered in the course of an ethnographic field study at a hair stylist's salon in a large Austrian city in April 2005. In this paper the hairdressing salon is referred to by the pseudonym Cutting Edge. For two consecutive weeks, I conducted participant observation at the shop for about four hours per day. I wrote field notes on site, which I expanded into observation protocols on the same or on the next day. I conducted qualitative interviews with three of the four hair stylists working there (one of the employees was on holiday at the time), including the owner. I collected artefacts produced by the hair stylists at the shop, such as coupons, advertisements, price lists, the website, and an album containing photographs of house-made hairstyles, which customers could look at to get ideas for their new haircut. Out of the data I collected during my field study, I will focus on the photographs of the house-made hairstyles available in the album and on the shop's website as well as on the observation protocols.

The data analysis was conducted within the methodological framework of multimodal discourse analysis (van Leeuwen 2005; Kress and van Leeuwen 2001) and focuses on hairstyles and interactions between customers and hairdressers in the saloon. For the analysis of hairstyles, I further relied on the method of artefact analysis as laid out by Manfred Lueger (2000) and Ulrike Froschauer (2002). Artefact analysis is an interpretative method. The term artefact refers to a materialized product of human acts. An artefact is a semiotic resource (van Leeuwen 2005: 3) and an object at the same time. As an object an artefact has a materiality that requires certain actions for its production and sets certain conditions to its use. Therefore, an artefact is also a materialization of the social circumstances under which it was produced and used (Lueger 2000: 141, 146f.). However, an artefact is also a semiotic resource, in other words, it is used to communicate and it is experienced as meaningful. It not only refers to the acts of the people who produced and used it, but also to the meanings that those people connected with their acts. People who share the same life world explicate these meanings in largely the same ways. Therefore, certain artefacts have roughly the same meanings for them (Schütz 1979: 39). For example, a punk knows that her hairstyle is considered as provocative by many, and many beholders will understand a punk hairstyle as a sign of protest – whether they sympathize with this form of protest or not.

Artefact analysis is a method of developing hypotheses about the life world in which artefacts exist. In an artefact analysis both aspects of the social context of an artefact are (re-)constructed: the collective structures of meaning that are apparent in the artefact as well as the system of acts in which it was produced and used. Methodically, this is achieved by translating the social context of the artefact into language. The challenge is to explore as many different (re-)constructions of its social context as possible. For that purpose the analysts have to use their extensive knowledge, which can come from everyday life or from the world of science and theory. The artefact is systematically examined from various perspectives in order to develop a broad understanding of the artefact's social context. The analysis does not have to follow a certain sequence, but it is helpful to begin with the description of the manifest aspects of the artefact and, from there, work towards the analysis of its more latent structures (Lueger 2000: 150f.). For this analysis, I started out with a definition of the research context that frames the interpretation of the artefact. As a second step, the artefact was deconstructed by dividing it into its constituent parts and by transcribing it into a field protocol. The more manifest meanings of the artefact in its social context were then reconstructed. The third and final step was the reconstruction of latent social structures that enable the production and use of the artefact.

Following Froschauer's (2002: 372-374) suggestions on quality assurance in artefact analysis, the analysis was conducted together with a fellow researcher. Froschauer recommends that the analyst group should have a diverse composition regarding the categories relevant to the research question. With regard to our project, the relevant differences are mainly those of gender and age. While the diversity requirement was met in terms of gender (with the other researcher being male), the two of us are, however, quite similar in terms of age (27 and 30 years of age).

The analysis of hairstyles was conducted on the basis of photographs. It did not focus on the photographs themselves, but treated them as transparent media that show hairstyles. In other words, the artefacts analyzed were the hairstyles, not the photographs. (An analysis of the photographs would have taken into account features like the selectivity of the displayed motif, the visual perspective, and so on.) The photographs were used as visual aids to refresh the researcher's memories and widen the database.

As a sample all the hairstyles shown on the website and in the house-made photo album available to customers at the shop were used. Apparently, these hairstyles were considered to be typical of the shop in the sense that the hair stylists use them as figureheads and representative advertisements aimed both at customers and at a larger public. Out of these, those hairstyles that qualified as graphic cuts according to the definition above were selected and analyzed further. There were 24 hairstyles presented on the website, 14 of which qualified as graphic cuts. The photo album contained pictures of 20 hairstyles. Five of them were no graphic cuts. Out of the 15 graphic cuts in the photo album, three were doublets that were also presented on the website. Thus altogether 26 different graphic cuts were analyzed.

In order to proceed with the analysis (Froschauer 2002; cf. Lueger 2000), the graphic cuts at Cutting Edge are contrasted with a comparable but different artefact often produced at a different type of hairdresser's salon: the dyed permanent wave. For this purpose, I draw on an ethnographic study conducted by Frida Kerner Furman in the US in 1991. The dyed permanent wave is an interesting point of reference, as it is considered the typical hairstyle of older women in Austria and other western countries, such as Great Britain and the United States. At Cutting Edge, the dyed permanent wave is usually referred to by the rather derogatory term "Omafrisur" ("granny hairstyle"); in the United Kingdom it has given name to the "blue rinse brigade"; and in US-American TV series we can find it on the head of numerous more or less appealing but often ridiculous older female characters.

It should be noted that the methodology explained above limits the generalisability of results to the scope of the examined cases, that is to say, to the particular hairdresser's salons. In order to claim wider generalisability, further research, for example ensuing case studies based on theoretical sampling, or a combination of textual analysis with quantitative methods, would be necessary.

In the following chapters I will first examine the layers of cultural meaning inherent in the dyed permanent wave and then proceed by analyzing the meaning of the graphic cut as well as its social contexts and conditions.

4 Restoring the Youthful Body: The Dyed Permanent Wave at Julie's International Salon

In her ethnographic study Kerner Furman conducted fieldwork at a hairdresser's during a period of eighteen months, using participant observation and informal interviewing as research tools (Kerner Furman 1997: 9). The hairdresser's, which she calls Julie's International Salon, is located in a large Midwestern city in the USA. It is a shop mainly frequented by Jewish women aged 50 and older. In contrast to Cutting Edge, it is a ladies only salon. It is run by the shop owner, Julie, who employs five female staff, all in their thirties, forties, and fifties; one of them is responsible for hair washing, three are beauticians, and one is a manicurist. The customers at Julie's International Salon use a common approach to ageing in that they do the best they can to retain their feminine beauty, and, in doing so, they conform to social expectations regarding acceptable self-presentation (Kerner Furman 1997: 110). The marks of ageing are commonly considered as unattractive.

Photograph 4: At Julie's International Salon (Kerner Furman 1997: 90)

At Julie's the hairdressers advise customers to dye their hair, assuring them that this will make them "look better". One customer explains: "We feel that our hair is very important, and it's the one thing we can still do something about. I can't do anything about the wrinkles; I can't do anything about the ... liver spots." (Kerner Furman 1997: 110)

It is considered the individual woman's responsibility to look feminine and beautiful. The body, including the hair, is seen as a material that can be designed at will. This freedom to modify the body, however, is offset by the social pressure to conform to norms of feminine beauty. Age is no longer an excuse for looking old (as it used to be in the discourse of age as inevitable decay). The hairdressers in turn encourage women to rely on practices such as dyeing that promise to improve the body. A woman who looks old, who "lets herself go" is seen as unvirtuous and potentially depressed.

The overall aim is not only to look younger, but also to look natural. Measures taken to appear younger must be hidden. Colouring the hair is acceptable, but it must not depart too much from common-sense reality. For example, it is considered as inappropriate and ridiculous if an older white woman dyes her hair pitch-black, as this is a natural impossibility. The aim is to look youthful, but not artificially youthful, or the women might give away her desperate need to stay looking young (Kerner Furman 1997: 116).

For the women at Julie's International Salon it is very important to wear age-appropriate hairstyles. Kerner Furman is recurrently told that she can wear her hair in the style she does because of her relatively young age, or, as the older women repeatedly assure her, because "you are young". (Kerner Furman 1997: 104). Dark hair is considered inappropriate on older women, while blond hair and a permanent wave are considered flattering. The underlying idea is that it is undesirable to see an older women's face. Dark hair is thought to call attention to the face and, therefore, to show the wrinkles. With a permanent the woman is thought to look better because "there is less face and more hair" (Kerner Furman 1997: 112).

The typical hairstyles produced at Julie's International Salon, such as the dyed permanent wave, can be understood as articulations of the self in the context of honour (cf. Allert 2004): It is important to look good, not to let oneself go, but not to overdo this by violating norms of modesty and naturalness.

Kerner Furman argues that to understand these women's actions, we first have to understand that women in this setting typically see themselves from the perspective of men. Older women, moreover, also see themselves from the perspective of a younger person.

> Hence [an older woman] is twice objectified, or, perhaps, more accurately in this instance, she partakes in the process of self-objectification in two ways: as woman and *old* woman. As woman she is observed by the internalized male gaze. As older woman she is observed by the internalized gaze of youth. We spot here another unequal social relation, which, like the male-female relation, is a relationship of dominance-subordination. (Kerner Furman 1997: 109)

Being an older woman is viewed so negatively at Julie's International Salon because older women are no longer objects of the – visual and otherwise – enjoyment of men. A woman's value is defined by the male gaze. For an older woman this implies a loss of social status, power, and affirmation. For this reason, she tries to preserve her youthful appearance as long a possible. However, the endeavour "is ultimately bound to fail because a woman cannot do enough to ensure that she looks young enough to garner respect and visibility" (Kerner Furman 1997: 113). Under these conditions, being an older woman is a sad fate.

5 Expressing Personality: The Graphic Cut at Cutting Edge

Cutting Edge is located in a large city in Austria. It is run by a female owner who employs three female hair stylists. The owner is in her forties, the other staff are in their twenties. One of them is a hairdresser's apprentice (a "Lehrling" according to the three stage system of craftsmanship in German-speaking countries); two are trained hairdressers ("Gesellen"), the owner is a master hairdresser ("Meister"). They prefer not to be called hairdressers ("Friseurinnen") but hair stylists, to emphasize the artistic character of their work. The customers are of mixed age and gender. The shop is well known in the city for its unusual and colourful graphic cuts and "posh punk creations", as one journalist has called them in a newspaper article.

On a material level the graphic cut consists of hair, which might have been dyed, and possibly also of shaven areas. The hair is very short, even though it can contain small sections of longer hair as parts of the pattern or image (e.g. a single braid, a pigtail, or long hair as the curtains besides a window that has been painted on the back of the head). These material elements have profound consequences: Short hair is quick to wash and style. It gives prominence to the face, which implies self-confidence and straightforwardness. Most importantly, it has traditional masculine connotations.

On a physical level, extremely short hair rules out a whole range of gestures that can be used to construct femininity (Budde 2004). Much more so than a man, a woman who wears a short hairstyle like the graphic cut subverts normative conceptions of gender and sexual orientation, which is why such hairstyles also have connotations of gay and lesbian culture. The egalitarian approach to gender is also evident in the pricing policy at Cutting Edge: While at most Austrian hairdresser's men pay lower prices, at Cutting Edge "prices are unisex, as closely calculated with regard to time and material consumed as possible" (from the Cutting Edge website).

The shaven areas are perhaps the most unusual and shocking element of the hairstyle. In contemporary western societies, being bald is only acceptable for men. But even for men the connotations of baldness are generally negative; it is associated with old age and sickness. Shaving is the most irreversible thing one can possibly do to one's hair. While colour can be dyed over, and longer hair can be cut shorter, with shaven areas the only option left is to shave off the remaining hair too, or to cover the head. Shaven areas are hard to change and hard to hide, which is why head shaving used to be a traditional form of punishment in Europe. To get one's head shaved, wholly or partially, is a temporarily irreversible and, therefore, quite courageous decision.

The colours of pattern cuts are, obviously, artificial. If no colours are used, it is the pattern or image that gives an obviously artificial, man-made impression. Graphic cuts are clearly recognizable as the results of creative acts. This obvious artificiality is what most strongly distinguishes them from traditional women's hairstyles. According to the ideal of traditional feminine beauty, a hairstyle should appear natural. It should only add delicate aesthetic emphasis. Despite manipulating the hair, women traditionally should keep up the semblance of naturalness (Budde 2004: 201). For an older woman with grey hair, dyeing her hair in flashy colours is very different from dyeing her hair in a seemingly natural colour: Flashy colours look blatantly artificial on people of all ages. This makes them a self-confident adornment, not a shameful attempt to imitate natural beauty. In this respect a graphic cut has some similarities with a baroque wig, which everyone knows to be artificial, but which is considered a decoration. This interpretation is further supported by the fact that some of the women who wear graphic cuts use their naturally grey hair as a canvass on which they then place patterns or images (see photographs 5 and 6). With their brilliant and unnatural colours, these hairstyles share some similarities with the deviant hairstyles worn by punks. However, the general impression of the Cutting Edge graphic cuts is a tidy one ("posh punk"), which distinguishes them from street punk style.

The hair, the colours, and the shaven areas are arranged into patterns or images. Here almost everything is possible: patterns that are reminiscent of animal furs, floral motives, modern works of art (e.g. pictures by Keith Haring – possibly also an allusion to gay culture – or by Pablo Picasso), humorous representational stageings (e.g. a sailboat, or the pope's pileolus at the time of the appointment of the new pope), and abstract compositions of colourful surfaces. The patterns and images can be used to express all sorts of feelings and moods: wild, strict, harmonious, merry, solemn, soft, hard, elegant, etc.

Graphic cuts are controversial. Different people associate different meanings with them. For somebody with an antipathy to graphic cuts, they may symbolize an unwillingness to integrate into society as well as a certain disrespect for tradition.

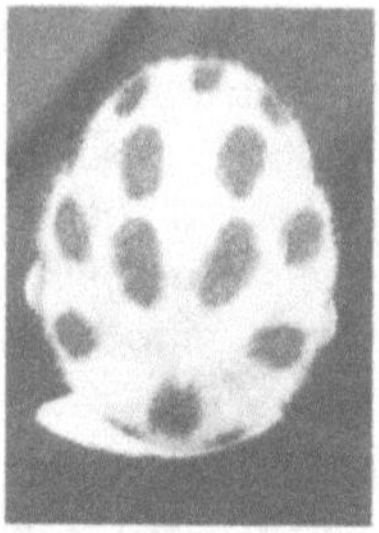

Photograph 5: Graphic cut with natural grey (1)

Photograph 6: Graphic cut with natural grey (2)

The wearer of a graphic cut may be suspected of violating traditional virtues, such as hard work, sense of family, demureness, and chastity. The gender blurring by women who wear graphic cuts may be considered as a threat to the family, a loss of femininity, and, therefore, as downright ugly. In a word, the graphic cut can be seen as a materialized threat to established society, possibly leading to social isolation, singularisation, loss of solidarity, and social impoverishment (cf. Huinik's and Wagner's summary of the criticism of individualization, 1998: 87).

What some people might criticize about flamboyant hairstyles such as the graphic cut is a positive feature in the eyes of the enthusiast. The graphic cut aims to express an oppositional attitude and to emphasise the wearer's individuality. With its almost indefinite possibilities of creating new patterns and images the graphic cut opposes the "uniform hairstyle", as the hair stylists at Cutting Edge call it, which is produced at other hairdresser's. Women who wear graphic cuts deliberately choose not to look like "good girls". The graphic cut does not dramatise gender and age; it is worn by young and old, male and female people alike. What counts is the expression of the individual's personality, not the adherence to social norms. If the hairstyles at Julie's International Salon are articulations of the self in the context of honour, graphic cuts are articulations of the self in the context of authenticity (Allert 2004). In this sense the conception of the self underlying the graphic cut is a romantic and modern one: Each person is seen to possess a true, authentic self, and life is a quest for establishing and fulfilling it (Potter and Wetherell 1987: 100). The hairstyle can be regarded as a medium for being oneself, for being authentic: The customer, with the support of the hair stylist, decides who she is and which hairstyle is most suitable for expressing her identity. It should be noted that the graphic cut, in spite of being considered unisex and uniage, still has distinctly masculine and youthful connotations. An older woman who gets a graphic cut knows that she is violating normative conceptions of feminine beauty and age-appropriate demeanour. It seems that in our society the demonstrative expression of the self with flashy, unusual hairstyles is, if at all, deemed most appropriate for young men (cf. Budde 2004).

When comparing the aesthetic appeal of conventional older women's hairstyles at Julie's International Salon, such as the dyed permanent, and that of graphic cuts, the difference is striking: The dyed permanent at Julie's is considered beautiful because it prolongs the appearance of youthfully thick, naturally coloured hair. It idealizes the beauty of the female body, for which there is only one fairly restrictive norm. The graphic cut, in contrast, is considered beautiful because it is a creative achievement and a courageous act. Above all, it is beautiful because it expresses the individual's personality. It idealizes the beauty of the wearer's personality, of which there are many positive realizations.

The emancipatory discourse of ageing that lies behind the graphic cut has large potential to make old age more liveable for women. If old age is conceptualized as decline, the older woman has lost immediately; she is considered an "old bag", a "shapeless, empty container, one which after use should simply be thrown away" (Kerner Furman 1997: 109). If a woman's aim is that of "successful ageing", she is considered to have the opportunity and duty to postpone this process of decline. However, the promise does not hold in the end, because she can never do enough to look young, and sooner or later she will find herself "declined" and deprived of respect and visibility. In the discourse of emancipated ageing a woman's value is not attached to her beauty, fitness, or activity, but to other qualities, such as courage, uniqueness, and beauty of personality. These are qualities that people can possess and develop at any age, in fact, until the last minute of their lives.

6 Conditions of Expressing Personality

The construction of the self, whether in the context of honour or in the context of authenticity, is not an individual but a social act. No matter if one chooses a dyed permanent wave or a graphic cut, this act of self- articulation is only successful if it is recognized in the intended way by others. The phenomenon of older women wearing graphic cuts can only arise and persist under certain conditions. This section aims to highlight some conditions that make the phenomenon possible. Insofar as the graphic cut worn by older women is an act of resistance against dominant norms of feminine beauty and age-appropriate demeanour as well as an expression of individual personality, these findings are of a wider relevance to emancipated ageing.

First of all, getting a graphic cut requires financial resources. The costs of graphic cuts start at about EUR 30 for a very simply pattern and no dyeing. Theoretically, there is no upper limit, but the more intricate and colourful graphic cuts that are most frequently chosen cost up to about EUR 170. A graphic cut without dyeing stays well-groomed for three to four weeks, with dyeing it lasts up to about six weeks. Thus, altogether, it is more expensive than a dyed permanent at a run-of-the-mill hairdresser's.

Next, the person has to be physically able to seek out a hair stylist who produces graphic cuts. Here the options in Austria are very limited. According to the hair stylists at Cutting Edge, there are about four or five hairdressers in the city who do graphic cuts for men and women. Additionally, there are several Turkish barbers' that serve graphic designs for beards and scalp hair to a young male Turkish clientele. For getting a graphic cut it is therefore advantageous to live in a large city, and, on a more general level, it is necessary to be physically mobile. The mobile hairdressers, who visit old people at home, in residential homes, or in hospitals, do not specialise in graphic cuts.

This also points to the third material condition: In order to get a graphic cut, the customer needs a hair stylist who is willing and able to give her one. Whilst this may sound trivial at first glance, it is actually crucial. Many of the customers at Cutting Edge are, in the words of the owner, "older ladies who don't want to be given a uniform haircut as soon as they turn 40" (by which she implies that this is the age when age discrimination at other hairdresser's starts). In an interview, she puts it the following way:

Owner:	I simply know that, let's say, 80% of hairdressers give ladies around 45 a uniform hairstyle. Or they... They are approached entirely differently. So there are simply... Certain hairstyles are simply taboo, yes, well, they are only given to young people, and the range of choices is becoming increasingly conservative. And this, of course, annoys a lot of these people, because they don't feel that old at all.
F. Maier:	Do you have something like a philosophy here, or ...?
Owner:	Get granny out of coma! [laughs]
F. Maier:	What? Get granny out of coma?
Owner:	[laughs] Or: You're retired anyway, now you've got a jester's licence[2]!

Emancipated ageing by wearing a graphic cut is based on acts of consumption and depends on a certain amount of wealth, mobility, and people who supply the necessary services and products.

The next hurdle arises when it comes to actually wearing an unconventional hairstyle in everyday life. Wearing the "wrong" hairstyle can have very unpleasant consequences in professional as well as in private life. In certain jobs, wearing a graphic cut would undermine one's professional credibility and could lead to serious consequences, possibly even to dismissal. A partner may not respond positively to the outlandish new look, as, for example, hinted at in the following dialogue observed at Cutting Edge: Here a woman, presumably in her early seventies, is not getting a graphic cut, but an "asymmetric haircut with blond strands".

2 The original German word is "Narrenfreiheit", verbatim "jester's freedom".

Customer: I have told all my friends that I will change. They said I should in any event tell my husband in advance, so he'll let me in again.
Hair stylist: Does he not want you to change?
Customer: Everything is wonderful with my husband.

In most cases, however, the shock effect is taken into account and intended by the customers who come to Cutting Edge for an unusual hairstyle, as evident, for example, in the following interaction:

> The hair stylist has finished cutting the customer's hair. The customer is a woman, presumably in her fifties. Her daughter has accompanied her and is now standing on the side watching. The hair stylist rubs hair wax into the customer's hair and makes it stand off her head at 90 degrees. The hair stylist, the customer, and her daughter giggle. The customer says, "Jakob will get a shock. He's gonna say, 'Mum, you are OLD! This hairstyle is not for you!'" The three women almost roll on the floor laughing. The hair stylist continues arranging the customer's hair in a spiky fashion.

The customers at Cutting Edge have a very distinct professional and educational background. The owner describes them in the following way: "Many people from the psychotherapist scene, […] creative people, many people from the social sector, but also architects, artists, musicians, […] therapists […]". The list could be elongated to include university students, who are aspiring to, and pensioners, who have retired from these kinds of professions. Such observations strongly suggest that unusual hairstyles, like graphic cuts, are only acceptable to older women belonging to a certain milieu, the so-called "individualized milieu" (Koppetsch and Maier 1998), in which values and norms of egalitarianism, self-realization, and autonomy predominate. In socio-structural terms, it consists of the new, educated upper middle class with an urban lifestyle, that is to say, it includes mainly university graduates and intellectuals (Koppetsch and Maier 1998: 148).

7 Conclusion

Our analysis strongly suggests that there is, in fact, a counter-discourse of old age, which could be labelled as "emancipated ageing". It is characterized by an emphasis on personality, individuality, and a certain resistance to dominant norms of age, gender, and sexual orientation. It can be read as a manifestation of the values and norms of egalitarianism, self-realization, and autonomy. While these norms are, of course, no fixed laws inherent in graphic cuts, they represent the common attitude with which these hairstyles are worn. Moreover, wearing a flamboyant hairstyle is not the only way of emancipated ageing. People enact emancipated ageing also in the way they talk, work, spend their free time, consume certain products, and so on.

The effects of an emancipatory discourse of old age on older women's lives, compared to those of discourses of decay and of "successful ageing", are potentially positive. With its emphasis on inner qualities, emancipated ageing opens a possibility of lifelong maintenance or growth, which more widespread discourses of old age as decay or as "successful ageing" do not offer.

However, enacting an emancipatory discourse of old age depends on certain conditions. Since emancipated ageing is based on acts of consumption such as getting a particular hairstyle at the hairdresser's, it requires wealth, mobility, and people who supply the necessary services and products. The most crucial condition, however, is social feasibility. The older woman needs to live in an environment where emancipated ageing, whether enacted through graphic cuts or other practices, is accepted. Evidence from this case study suggests that, at least as far as graphic cuts are concerned, the prevalence of emancipated ageing is limited to a privileged social milieu, namely that of the new, educated urban middle class.

Literature

Allert, T. (2004): Transitorische Prominenz - Gestaltungsoptionen und Gestaltungsrestriktionen in der Haarpflege. Haar tragen: Eine kulturwissenschaftliche Annäherung. Janecke, Christian. Köln, Böhlau Verlag: 99-108.

Biggs, S. (2001): Toward critical narrativity: stories of aging in contemporary social policy. Journal of Ageing Studies 15: 303-316.

Budde, J. (2004): Interaktion und Distinktion. Haarpraktiken bei Schülern. Haar tragen: Eine kulturwissenschaftliche Annäherung. Janecke, Christian. Köln, Böhlau Verlag: 195-208.

Butler, J. (1990): Gender Trouble: Feminism and the Subversion of Identity. New York and London, Routledge.

Butler, J. (2004): Undoing Gender. New York, Routledge.

Casalanti, T. (2005): Ageism, Gravity, and Gender: Experiences of Ageing Bodies. Generations XXIX(3): 8-12.

Coupland, J. (2007): Gendered discourses on the "problem" of ageing: consumerized solutions. Discourse & Communication 1(1): 37-61.

Coupland, J. and Williams, A. (2002): Conflicting discourses, shifting ideologies: pharmaceutical, 'alternative' and feminist emancipatory texts on the menopause. Discourse & Society 13(4): 419-445.

Coupland, N., Coupland, J. and Giles, H. (1989): Telling age in later life: Identity and face implications. Text 9(2):129-151.

Cruikshank, M. (2003): Learning to be old: gender, culture, and ageing. Lanham, Md. et al., Rowman & Littlefield.

Foucault, M. (1972): The Archaeology of Knowledge. London, Tavistock.

Froschauer, U. (2002): Artefaktanalyse. Methoden der Organisationsforschung. Kühl, S. and Strodtholz, P. Reinbek, rororo: 361-395.

Garfinkel, H. (1967): Studies in Ethnomethodology. Englewood Cliffs, NJ, Prentice Hall.

Gubrium, J.F., Holstein, J.A. and Buckholt, D.R. (1994): Constructing the life course. Dix Hills, NY, General Hall.

Holstein, M. (1997): Alzheimer's Disease and Senile Dementia, 1885-1920: An Interpretive History of Disease Negotiation. Journal of Aging Studies 11(1): 1-13.

Huinik, J. and Wagner, M. (1998): Individualisierung und die Pluralisierung von Lebensformen. In: Friedrichs, J. (ed.): Die Individualisierungs-These. Opladen, Leske + Budrich: 85-106.

Janecke, Ch. (2004): Einleitung - Haar tragen. In: Janecke, Ch. (ed.): Haar tragen: Eine kulturwissenschaftliche Annäherung. Köln, Böhlau Verlag: 3-48.

Kerner Furman, F. (1997): Facing the Mirror: Older Women and Beauty Shop Culture. New York and London, Routledge.

Koppetsch, C. and Maier, M.S. (1998): Individualisierung ohne Gleichheit? Zur aktuellen Lage des Geschlechterverhältnisses. In: Friedrichs, J. (ed.): Die Individualisierungs-These. Opladen, Leske + Budrich: 144-164.

Kress, G. and van Leeuwen, T. (2001): Multimodal Discourse: The Modes and Media of Contemporary Communication. London, Arnold.

Laliberte Rudman, D. (2006): Shaping the active, autonomous and responsible modern retiree: an analysis of discursive technologies and their links with neo-liberal political rationality. Ageing & Society 26(181-201).

Leibing, A. (2005): The old lady from Ipanema: Changing notions of old age in Brazil. Journal of Ageing Studies 19(15-31).

Lin, M.-C., Hummert, M.L. and Harwood, J. (2004): Representation of age identities in on-line discourse. Journal of Ageing Studies 18: 261-274.

Lueger, M. (2000): Grundlagen qualitativer Forschung. Wien, WUV.

McHugh, K.H. (2000): The "Ageless Self"? Emplacement of Identities in Sun Belt Retirement Communities. Journal of Aging Studies 14(1): 103-115.

Morganroth Gullette, M. (1997): Declining to decline: Cultural combat and the politics of midlife. Charlottesville, VA, University Press of Virginia.

Potter, J. and Wetherell, M. (1987): Discourse and Social Psychology: Beyond Attitudes and Behaviour. London, Sage.

Potts, A., Grace, V.M., Vares, T. and Gavey, N. (2006): "Sex for life"? Men's counter-stories on "erectile dysfunction", male sexuality and ageing. Sociology of Health & Illness 28(3): 306–329.

Sankar, A. (1984): It's Just Old Age: Old Age as a Diagnosis in American and Chinese Medicine. In: Kertzer, D.I. and Keith J. (eds.): Age and Anthropological Theory. London, Cornell University Press: 250-280.

Schütz, A. (1979): Strukturen der Lebenswelt, Band 1. Frankfurt am Main, Suhrkamp Verlag.

Sinding, Ch. and Gray, R. (2005): Active aging - spunky survivorship? Discourses and experiences of the years beyond breast cancer. Journal of Ageing Studies 19: 147-161.

Trethewey, A. (2001): Reproducing and Resisting the Master Narrative of Decline. Management Communication Quarterly 15(2): 183-226.

Tulle-Winton, E. (1999): Growing old and resistance: Towards a new cultural economy of old age? Ageing & Society 19: 281-299.

van Leeuwen, T. (2005): Introducing Social Semiotics. London and New York, Routledge.

West, C. and Zimmerman, D.H. (1987): Doing gender. Gender & Society 1(2): 125-151.

Authors, Editors, and the Artist

Aaltio, Iiris

Dr. Iiris Aaltio is professor at University of Jyväskylä, School of Business and Economics. Her research work covers issues on organization culture, leadership and gender, and has been published in several journals like Organizational Change Management and Human Relations. She is co-editor of the books "Gender, Identity and the Culture of Organizations" (2002) and "Women Entrepreneurship and Social Capital. A dialogue and construction" (2008).
Email: iiris.aaltio @ econ.jyu.fi

Beisheim, Margret

Dipl.-Oec. Dr.^{in} Margret Beisheim was born in 1950 in Kassel/Germany. She did an apprenticeship as an industrial clerk, worked for almost ten years as a secretary in German industrial companies and studied work science as well as economics and business administration at the University of Hannover, Germany. For more than a decade she has been working as a lecturer at the Institute for Human Resource Management at Vienna University of Economics and Business Administration (WU Wien). 1999-2002 she was Head of Department for HRM at the University of Applied Sciences and Technologies in Salzburg/Austria, Faculty of Information Business. Since 2002 she is assistant professor at WU Wien, Institute for HRM. She also works as a trainer, consultant and coach and as a lecturer at *FHWien University of Applied Sciences of WKW* in the Master's programme in Hospitality & Tourism Management.
Email: margret.beisheim @ wu-wien.ac.at

von Bonsdorff, Monika

M. Sc. (Econ.) Monika von Bonsdorff is a researcher at the Finnish Institute of Occupational Health. She graduated with a Masters degree in Management and Leadership in 2004 from the University of Jyväskylä, School of Business and Economics, and is currently writing her doctoral thesis on rewarding aging nurses. Her study interests include rewarding different aged employees, organizational justice, early retirement and bridge employment, workability and company performance. Monika von Bonsdorff has attended a number of international and national conferences and she has several publications in the field of management.
Email: monika.bonsdorff @ econ.jyu.fi

Clarke, Marilyn

Dr. Marilyn Clarke is a senior lecturer in the School of Management at the University of South Australia. Her research interests include the changing nature of work and careers, career transitions (particularly the effects of taking voluntary redundancy) and the management of employability. She teaches in the areas of HRM and Change Management.
Email: clarke.marilyn @ unisa.edu.au

Eberherr, Helga

Mag.[a] Helga Eberherr is a sociologist and researcher at the Research Institute for Gender & Diversity in Organizations at Vienna University of Economics and Business Administration. She is also a lecturer at the University of Vienna.
Email: helga.eberherr @ wu-wien.ac.at

Fleischmann, Alexander

Mag. Alexander Fleischmann studied International Business Administration at the University of Vienna and the Swedish School of Economics and Business Administration in Helsinki. After working as a research assistant in the EQUAL project AGEpowerment he is currently a research and teaching assistant at the Academic Unit for Gender & Diversity Management at Vienna University of Economics and Business Administration.
Email: alexander.fleischmann @ wu-wien.ac.at

Gusenbauer, Bianca

MMag.[a] Dr.[in] Bianca Gusenbauer is currently a scholarship holder at the University of Economics in Prague and a lecturer at the Vienna University of Economics and Business Administration. Her primary research interests are infrastructure finance, poverty reduction and foreign exchange rate management. Before she has worked for four years as a research and teaching assistant at the Institute for International Business at the WU Wien and as a lecturer at several European Universities. She earned her doctoral degree in 2007 and her master's degree in 2003, both from the WU Wien. Bianca Gusenbauer has attended a number of international and national conferences and has publications in the field of Business Administration.
Email: bianca.gusenbauer @ wu-wien.ac.at

Hartmann, Linley

Dr. Linley Hartmann is an adjunct senior researcher at the School of Management at the University of South Australia and frequently is a visiting professor at the WU-Wien. Her initial research interests in older workers have broadened to

include all aspects of International Human Resource Management including how contextual factors create subtle differences in the similarities that influence options for individuals. She has published specifically on these topics and more generally on Human Resource Management in books and journals.
Email: linley.hartmann @ unisa.edu.au

Hofmann, Roswitha

Mag.[a] Roswitha Hofmann is a faculty member of the Department of Management – Academic Unit for Gender & Diversity Management at Vienna University of Economics and Business Administration. Her main fields of research are knowledge and competence in organizations from a gender and diversity perspective.
Email: roswitha.hofmann @ wu-wien.ac.at

Kloimüller, Irene

Dr.[in] Irene Kloimüller is management consultant (specialised on age-management, stress, mobbing, health promotion), personnel consultant, trainer and coach. She works as a senior consultant at IBG – Institut für humanökologische Unternehmensführung, Vienna. (www.ibg.co.at) and is a member of the ViA Coaching Network. Her educational background: study of Medicine, psychotherapist, postgraduate studies in Business Administration and Health Care Management
Email: irene.kloimueller @ chello.at

Koponen, Sirpa

MA Sirpa Koponen works as a project manager for the Advanced Management Education Centre of the University of Jyväskylä. She graduated with a master's degree in organizational communication in 2004 from the Department of Communication, University of Jyväskylä. Currently she is continuing her doctoral studies of leadership and management at the School of Business and Economics, University of Jyväskylä. Her study interests include age management and leadership styles and their effects on organizational justice, organizational commitment, job satisfaction and early retirement.
Email: sirpa.koponen @ cec.jyu.fi

Kreil, Linda

Mag.[a] Dr.[in] Linda Kreil studied law and worked as a research assistant at the department for trade/commerce law and economic law at the Salzburg University. She graduated with a thesis on employment law in groups of companies published in 1996. After her practice time at several Viennese Courts of Justice she worked at the Kunz Schima Wallentin law firm in Vienna mainly in the fields of economic law and employment law, afterwards at the Griesser Gerlach Gahleitner law firm specialising in employment law. Since 2003 she is an assistant professor at the

Institute for Austrian and European Labour Law and Social Law at Vienna University of Economics and Business Administration (WU Wien). She researches and publishes mainly in the field of employment law, e.g. about holidays/ vacation in the period of notice, leave of absence in the time of terminal care, age discrimination in the employment relationship, and the employment law and social law under conditions of globalisation and flexibility.
Email: linda.kreil @ wu-wien.ac.at

Maier, Florentine

Mag.^{a} Dr.^{in} Florentine Maier is a research assistant at the Institute for Nonprofit Management at Vienna University of Economics and Business Administration (WU Wien). Her primary research interests are the employment of older workers and the spread of managerialism into nonprofit organisations. Before, she worked as a research assistant at the Institute of Human Resource Management at WU Wien, as a lecturer in human resource management at the University of Applied Sciences of WKW, and as a Chinese teacher for BIKU MTI. She earned a doctoral degree in Social and Economic Sciences from WU Wien in 2008.
Email: florentine.maier @ wu-wien.ac.at

Mayerhofer, Helene

Mag.^{a} Dr.^{in} Helene Mayerhofer is associate professor at the Institute for Human Resource Management at Vienna University of Economics and Business Administration (WU Wien). Her research interests include all aspects of International Human Resource Management, especially the consequences of non-standard international assignments (e.g. flexpatriates) for individuals and organisations. This encompasses career, work-life-balance, and human resource management involvement. She has published specifically on these topics and more generally on human resource management in books and journals like the Zeitschrift für Personalforschung, International Journal of Human Resource Management, and Thunderbird International Business Review.
Email: helene.mayerhofer @ wu-wien.ac.at

Patrickson, Margaret

Dr. Margaret Patrickson is an adjunct associate professor at the International Graduate School of Business with the University of South Australia where her role is largely supervision of doctoral candidates in the university's outreach program within South East Asia and occasional input into the doctoral program. Though her research interests have been dominated by research into older workers she has also published in all fields of human resource management including four books and over twenty journal articles.
Email: margaret.patrickson @ unisa.edu.au

Znojemsky, Greta

MMag.[a] Greta Znojemsky was born in Vienna. Studies at the University of Applied Arts and the Academy of Fine Arts in Vienna. Scholarship in Paris. 1993: Founding of the 'Windspiel Laboratory for Creativity and Treasure Hunting®', a training centre and studio for research into the relationship between creativity and personality development. 2001: Founding of the Windspiel Gallery, a platform for national and inter-cultural projects. Since 1982, solo exhibitions and participation in group displays in Austria, Peru, USA, Russia, Israel, France, Sweden, Uzbekistan, Palestine and Germany. Workshops in Austria, Greece, Italy, Peru, Uzbekistan and Palestine. Work on show in public and private collections in Austria, Germany, Finland, Peru, Australia, Uzbekistan and Palestine. Co-founder and president (since 2001) of Kunstart-Europäisches Kunstnetzwerk. Member of IG Bildende Kunst, of eop - Emergence of Projects, and of IAPMA, International Association of Hand Papermakers and Paper Artists. Curator and exhibition organiser for national and international projects. Works at the interface between art and everyday life.

Email: greta @ windspiel.at; www.greta.znojemsky.windspiel.at

Old Woman (2)
Linoleum Stencil

Frauen, Forschung und Wirtschaft

Herausgegeben von Regine Bendl, Karin Heitzmann
und Angelika Schmidt

Band 1-6 sind von 1991-1996 im Service Fachverlag, Wien erschienen.

Band 7 Ursula Marianne Ernst / Luise Gubitzer / Angelika Schmidt (Hg.): Ökonomie M(m)acht Angst. Zum Verhältnis von Ökonomie und Religion. 1997.

Band 8 Renate Buber / Ursula Marianne Ernst (Hrsg.): Frauenwege. An einer Wirtschaftsuniversität zwischen Politik und Wissenschaft. 1999.

Band 9 Johanna Hofbauer / Ursula Doleschal / Ludmila Damjanova (Hrsg.): Sosein – und anders. Geschlecht, Sprache und Identität. 1999.

Band 10 Erna Nairz-Wirth / Gabriele Michalitsch (Hrsg.): FrauenArbeitsLos. 2000.

Band 11 Karin Heitzmann / Angelika Schmidt (Hrsg.): Frauenarmut. Hintergründe, Facetten, Perspektiven. 2001. 2., durchgesehene Auflage 2002.

Band 12 Gabriele Michalitsch / Erna Nairz-Wirth (Hrsg.): Frauen – Außer Konkurrenz? 2002.

Band 13 Margit Appel / Luise Gubitzer / Birgit Sauer (Hrsg.): Zivilgesellschaft – ein Konzept für Frauen? 2003.

Band 14 Karin Heitzmann / Angelika Schmidt (Hrsg.): Wege aus der Frauenarmut. 2004.

Band 15 Luise Gubitzer / Birgit Trukeschitz (Hrsg.): Frauen und Budget. 2004.

Band 16 Evelyn Dawid: 6668 und eine Wirtschaftsakademikerin. Ein Einzelporträt in Worten, ein Gruppenporträt in Zahlen. 2005.

Band 17 Luise Gubitzer / Susanne Schunter-Kleemann (Hrsg.): Gender Mainstreaming – Durchbruch der Frauenpolitik oder deren Ende? Kritische Reflexion einer weltweiten Strategie. 2006.

Band 18 Margret Beisheim / Florentine Maier / Linda Kreil / Bianca Gusenbauer (eds.): Constructions of Women's Age at the Workplace. 2009.

www.peterlang.de

FSC
www.fsc.org
MIX
Papier | Fördert gute Waldnutzung
FSC® C083411

Kolibri 360 GmbH
Ferdinand-Jühlke-Straße 7
99095 Erfurt, Deutschland
produktsicherheit@kolibri360.de

Druck:
CPI Druckdienstleistungen GmbH
im Auftrag der
Kolibri 360 GmbH
Ferdinand-Jühlke-Str. 7
99095 Erfurt